Understanding Child Psychopathology Through Fairytales

Alessandra Sax
Editor

Understanding Child Psychopathology Through Fairytales

palgrave
macmillan

Editor
Alessandra Sax
Athens, Greece

ISBN 978-3-032-14096-8 ISBN 978-3-032-14097-5 (eBook)
https://doi.org/10.1007/978-3-032-14097-5

This Palgrave Macmillan imprint is published by the registered company Springer Nature Switzerland AG.
The registered company address is: Gewerbestrasse 11, 6330 Cham, Switzerland

This book is dedicated to all the children around the world who have shown courage and resilience in the face of adversity in life, with or without their parents and/or caregivers.

I am especially grateful to my own parents—my father Barry and mother Angel—who provided me with unconditional love and encouragement throughout my childhood, adolescence, and adulthood. Both have illustrated that kindness, generosity, and love are what make the world a better place and that family matters (to my siblings: Lori, Eric, Craig, and Britt) and that all goals are reachable in life—with hard work, discipline, and passion.

And to my husband James and son James Craig, who guide my creative inclination and continue to support my every dream and vision—in serving others, always with a strong mind, heart, and spirit.

Foreword

In contemporary mental health education, where clinical knowledge often risks becoming detached from lived experience, this book offers a timely and original contribution. *Understanding Child Psychopathology Through Fairy Tales* bridges the domains of symbol, narrative, and developmental science in a way that is both pedagogically grounded and clinically resonant.

Conceived and guided by Dr. Alessandra Sax, this project grew out of an undergraduate course in Child Psychopathology. Rather than simply learning diagnostic criteria, students were invited to enter the emotional landscapes of children—fictional yet symbolically rich—through the medium of fairy tales. The result is a collection of case-based narratives in which each character becomes a canvas for exploring trauma, attachment, developmental disruption, and resilience.

Fairy tales and myths have long held a significant place in the symbolic and psychotherapeutic understanding of the human condition. From their origins in oral tradition, they have functioned as communal containers of meaning, encoding existential dilemmas, developmental crises, and archetypal struggles. Psychoanalytic thinkers such as Carl Jung, Bruno Bettelheim, Marie-Louise von Franz, and Clarissa Pinkola Estés have emphasized the symbolic depth of mythic and folkloric material as it relates to the psyche's individuation and integration processes. Bettelheim, in particular, in his seminal work, *The Uses of Enchantment* (1976), argued that fairy tales speak directly to the unconscious of the child, offering models for navigating fear, loss, rage, and transformation.

In the context of Greek culture, myth has always been more than a narrative. It has been ontology, cosmology, and pedagogy. From the tragedies of Aeschylus to the therapeutic work of contemporary Greek psychotherapists, myth continues to function as a framework for self-understanding and collective memory. Therapeutic schools in Greece, such as those influenced by archetypal psychology or integrative approaches, often incorporate mythic material to access symbolic dimensions of psychic life. Within this tradition, fairy tales occupy a bridging role: more accessible than high mythology, yet still rich in archetypal structure and emotional truth. This book stands within that lineage, adapting timeless narrative structures to the clinical understanding of the suffering child.

What also stands out in this work is its invitation to an interdisciplinary gaze. While grounded in clinical psychology, the text draws on literary analysis, developmental theory, and cultural narrative. This blending of domains enriches our understanding of the child—not only as a subject of diagnosis but also as a meaning-making being shaped by myth, metaphor, and memory.

As a psychologist and external reader of this project, I was deeply impressed by the intellectual curiosity and emotional sensitivity with which these emerging clinicians approached their task. Characters such as Dumbo, Peter Pan, Red Riding Hood, and Ariel are not treated reductively but are encountered with care and depth. Their symbolic content is translated into psychodynamic formulations, clinical hypotheses, and intervention strategies—without stripping them of their imaginative vitality.

This book also reaffirms a vital dimension of psychoanalytic pedagogy: the capacity to think symbolically and tolerate ambiguity. As Donald Winnicott reminded us, true learning occurs in transitional space—in the place where fantasy and reality meet, where thinking and feeling are not yet split. The use of fairy tales here is not a whimsical detour but a rigorous clinical exercise in empathy, attunement, and the search for meaning.

Dr. Sax and her students have offered us more than a training manual. They have modeled a way of thinking and teaching that deserves to be taken seriously across institutions. I encourage readers to approach this volume not only for its clinical insights but also as an invitation: to listen more deeply to the coded messages of children, and to honor the stories—real or imagined—that shape their inner worlds.

University of South Wales
United Kingdom
European Institute of Counseling and
Psychotherapy, Crete, Greece

Theodoros Tsirigotis

Preface

"Fairytales are culturally bound stories that serve as the means of preserving and passing on cultural values and collective identity"
~ Jaime Bergum

This project stemmed from a course I taught with undergraduate students at the Hellenic American College in Greece. As a clinician working for over 30 years with children and adolescents, the course Child Psychopathology is one of my favorites to teach. Since the course caters to understanding diagnostic categories and criteria for child and adolescent mental disorders, I aimed to find a topic for the final assessment that aligned with course objectives but was also creative, fun, and allowed students to think "outside of the box."

Combining narrative literature, symbols, and metaphors was an avenue in which fairytales were deemed to be a perfect fit for students to utilize their critical thinking skills, synthesize theory, and clinical case conceptualizations of a chosen character that exemplified his or her development among classic stories. Additionally, as fairytales are representative of our own childhood experiences—told orally or read to us—paralleling the fictitious character with the factual child (the client in this case for the purpose of the assessment) was my prominent thought process.

Furthermore, a fairytale is a symbolic place, usually the first that is introduced to a young child, to a world culturally encoded with social experiences and worldviews communicated from one generation to the next in our emerging selves (Chudnovskaya & Lipatova, 2020). According to Chudnovskaya and Lipatova (2020), psychologists such as Franz (2004), Fromm (2011), and Jung (1991) often wrote about the role of fairytales and myths in the formation of personality. In particular, character archetypes are essential components of fairytale variations.

As Western fairytales may be most familiar to us, such as those written in the seventeenth century by Charles Perrault (1697) and over 100 years later written by the Brothers Grimm (1818), a myriad of variations of these stories surpass cultural boundaries over the centuries. Taking into consideration the uniqueness of cultural contexts, character archetypes such as the wicked stepmother, fairy godmother, villain, princess, hero, sidekick, or trickster, differences in plot, character, and moral highlights (serving as a medium for teaching ethical principles and values), fairytales must adapt to the evolving needs and norms of each society across cultures and generations (Bergum, 2022).

Fairytales are real-world abstractions and interpretations of problems, problem-solving, and understanding of the trials and tribulations of life; they are both boundless in time and age. Fairytales are a phenomenon of the culture of human beings and preserve socio-economic structures, language, religion, values, beliefs, and overall cognition of our worldviews, alongside both our individual and collective identities. With chimeric influences, symbolic narratives, and archetypal imagery, fairytales are the perfect repository to reinforce and propagate ideals in children.

As you read through the following pages, the stories depicted are creative and symbolic in nature for pedagogic purposes, and by no means should be interpreted literally. Join in the diverse histories of the represented fairytale characters, dive into your own unique childhood, and let your imagination take you through the complexities of life.

Athens, Greece — Alessandra Sax

References

Bergum, J. (2022). Nostalgic to my childhood, symbolic to your culture: Discussing the intercultural adaptation of culturally bound fairy tales, MacEwan University. *Student eJournal*, *6*(1). https://doi.org/10.31542/muse.v6i1.2280

Chudnovskaya, I. N., & Lipatova, M. E. (2020). The fairy tale as a place of memory in the context of intergenerational communication. *Journal of History Culture and Art Research*, *9*(3), 178–186. https://doi.org/10.7596/taksad.v9i3.2824

Febiyanti, A., & Rachmawati, Y. (2020). *Is authoritative parenting the best parenting style? In Proceedings of the 5th International Conference on Early Childhood Education (ICECE 2020)* (pp. 94–99). Atlantis Press.
Obidjonovna, R. N. (2025). Different variations of traditional fairy tales and their components. *European International Journal of Philological Sciences*, *5*(3), https://eipublication.com/index.php/eijps

Acknowledgments I am thankful to my mentors, colleagues, students, and clients who have believed in the work I do over the many years of my personal and professional journey. You have motivated me to always be the best version of myself, even during difficult times in life.

I am so proud of my former undergraduate students who have contributed to this book. Thank you for your hard work, diligence, and commitment to the vision of this book.

I would especially like to thank Anna Rombotis for being a champion assistant throughout the development of this book and for her scholarly contributions. Her belief in the project, patience, and calming energy were truly inspiring.

An enormous thank you to Evgenia Boutsiarakos for her dedication to proofread and edit the manuscript, as my second pair of eyes during the final stage of this project. Her excellence in literary knowledge is to be commended.

Competing Interests There is no apparent direct competitor to this book, in that it combines the use of metaphor and fairytales in literature, alongside the DSM-V, utilized for informed pedagogy. The fictional characters are creatively analyzed to illustrate case conceptualizations of developmental psychopathology and serve as a training resource for counselor education in clinical practice. Narrative-driven tools appear to be lacking as resources for emerging clinicians and foster critical thinking skills in powerful, emotional, and thoughtful ways.

Disclaimer

The purpose of this book is for educational practice, to facilitate critical thinking about case conceptualizations for students and developing practitioners in the mental health field. By no means are the DSM-5 (2013) Childhood and Adolescent Diagnostic Criteria and Diagnoses, represented as accurate interpretations of the presented disorders of the characters. The chapters in this book represent only one lens of many in understanding childhood developmental psychopathology that serves merely for pedagogical and symbolic purposes—rather than literal. Cultural heritage should also be considered when interpreting fairytales to avoid stereotypes in individualistic or collectivistic cultures.

Contents

1 **Theoretical Introduction** 1
Alessandra Sax

2 **Dumbo the Elephant** 21
Anna Rombotis

3 **Little Red Riding Hood** 33
Anna Rombotis and Stella Kossidi

4 **Pinocchio** 45
Aysan Jahankhah and Anna Rombotis

5 **Hansel and Gretel** 55
Grace Zografaki and Anna Rombotis

6 **Peter Pan** 67
Aikaterini Avgerinou and Anna Rombotis

7 **The Little Mermaid: Ariel** 79
Sara Eleni Pliacha and Anna Rombotis

8 **Robin Hood** 91
Ioulia Fatourou and Anna Rombotis

Epilogue 105

Companion Guide for Educators 107

Developmental Psychopathology 109

Typical Versus Atypical Development 111

Developmental Models 113

Mental Health Challenges in Children and Adolescents 115

Companion Guide for Students and Trainees: Child and Adolescent Development, Psychopathology, and Related Models 117

Practice Guide of Ego Functions and Defense Mechanisms 123

Glossary 125

Recommended Reading 131

Notes on Contributors

Aikaterini Avgerinou is a psychology graduate from Hellenic American University (Class of 2022), holding a BSc in Psychology. She completed her psychology internship at the Children's Oncology Unit "Marianna V. Vardinoyannis—ELPIDA," gaining meaningful experience in clinical, pediatric, and child-focused environments. She has supported unaccompanied refugee children through her work with The Home Project, providing computer and English skills while applying psychological principles to offer guidance and emotional support. She has also contributed to Best Buddies Greece, promoting social inclusion for individuals with intellectual and developmental disabilities. Aikaterini is an active volunteer with The Smile of the Child, contributing across various organizational initiatives to support children and families in need. Passionate about child development, mental health, and social impact, she combines her academic training with meaningful practical experience to positively contribute to her community.

Ioulia Fatourou is a clinical psychologist with undergraduate and graduate training from Hellenic American University, Athens. She has collaborated with professionals across diverse areas of psychology, gaining solid experience in human development, emotion, and cognition. Her clinical work with children during her internship further shaped her therapeutic orientation. She maintains her private practice in Athens, where she works with adults.

Aysan Jahankhah is a mental health counseling professional based in New York, practicing under her Limited Permit (MHC-LP). She earned dual master's degrees—the Master of Arts and Master of Education in Mental Health Counseling—from Teachers College, Columbia University, where she focused on psychodynamic therapy, multicultural counseling, and resilience research. She also holds a Bachelor of Science in Psychology from Hellenic American College, graduating with strong foundations in research, assessment, and evidence-based clinical practice. Aysan provides individual psychotherapy to adults from diverse cultural and linguistic backgrounds, integrating psychodynamic, cognitive-behavioral, and trauma-informed approaches. She works as a psychotherapist at Therapeutic Experience and Peaceful Psychotherapy, New York, and as a counselor at Elev8 Center, New Jersey, where she supports clients navigating addiction recovery, emotional regulation, trauma, and major life transitions. Beyond her clinical roles, Aysan contributes to global mental health advocacy as a UN NGO Representative with the Global Emergency Response and Assistance (GERA). Her professional interests include resilience, migrant mental health, the integration of culturally grounded therapeutic practices, and equitable access to psychosocial support for displaced populations. Aysan is fluent in English, Persian, Greek, and Azerbaijani, and adopts a culturally attuned, client-centered approach to her therapeutic work.

Stella Kossidi is a psychology graduate from Hellenic American University (Class of 2021), holding a BSc in Psychology. She completed her bachelor thesis based on pets and well-being: pet owners, non-pet owners, and stress. She has completed many hours of volunteer work in various organizations. These include Sxedia, which supports people experiencing homelessness, poverty, and social exclusion through the sale of magazines, with all proceeds donated to those in need. She has also volunteered at GNI–Hatzikosta, an organization that assists individuals facing addiction to opioids and alcohol by providing withdrawal support, psychosocial assistance, motivation, and referrals to rehabilitation centers. In addition, she has contributed to Best Buddies, which empowers adults with neurodevelopmental difficulties such as intellectual disabilities, individuals on the autism spectrum, and those with Down syndrome. She has also offered her services at a homeless feeding center, Caritas, which accommodates up to 400 people and provides shelter, food supplies, psychological support, and medical care. Furthermore, she volunteered at Ison Psychometrical, an organization specializing in career counseling, human resources selection, development, and empowerment. Finally, she volunteered with Boroume ("We Can"), a non-profit organization dedicated to reducing food waste and addressing food insecurity in Greece. Stella is volunteering at a veterinary clinic as a secretary, where she supports both pet owners and their pets. Her duties include greeting clients, checking in patients, maintaining organization throughout the clinic, updating client and patient records, and managing paperwork and documentation. She integrates her bachelor's thesis on pet care with her volunteer work by observing daily clinical practices, collecting relevant insights, and applying theoretical knowledge to real-world interactions with animals and their owners.

Sara Pliacha is an American Greek clinical psychologist based in Athens, Greece. She is part of the Roots Wellness Center team and provides bilingual therapy for adults, with a clinical focus on Attention Deficit Hyperactivity Disorder (ADHD) and grief. Her work integrates evidence-based and person-centered approaches to support clients in managing attention-related difficulties, processing loss, and improving daily functioning.

Anna Rombotis is a psychology graduate of Hellenic American University, where she completed her degree as the highest-ranking student of her cohort (Summa Cum Laude). Her academic pathway began at the University of Edinburgh, supported by an exceptional IB score, before continuing in Athens. During her studies, she served as vice president of the Psychology Club and received the President's Leadership Award in recognition of her leadership and contributions to student initiatives. Anna completed her internship at Green Chimneys, New York, where she supported children with special needs through educational, nature-based, and animal-assisted activities. Her professional interests integrate psychological insight with creativity, evident in both her writing work and her commitment to community service. She has supported environmental and animal welfare efforts through organizations such as Sadhana Forest India and various Greek NGOs. In recent years, she has also cultivated expertise in vegan, plant-based cooking, approaching culinary practice as a creative, holistic extension of well-being and care.

Alessandra Sax holds a bachelor's degree in Psychology and Child Development from Hampshire College, United States. She graduated from New York University, United States, with a clinical master's degree in clinical social work, children, adolescents, and adults and completed her doctoral degree in Counseling Psychology and Supervision in Counselor Education at Argosy University, United States. She has been an instructor in Instructional Consultation, Clinical Interviewing and Consultation, Child Psychopathology, Child-Centered Play Therapy, Life-Span Development, Multicultural Perspectives, Cultural Psychology, Abnormal Psychology, Advanced Psychopathology, and Group and Music Therapy. She is also a licensed psychotherapist who has been in private practice for over 30 years, working with children, adolescents, and adults. Sax also acts as a consulting psychologist for various organizations. From 2006 to 2019, she worked at the American Community Schools of Athens (ACS), as the Elementary School Counselor and then School Psychologist, and additionally was the coordinator of the Psychology Intern Program within the Department of Student Affairs. During 2017–2022, Sax was the Co-Founder and Director of Learning and Wellness Center, a holistic therapeutic center for children, adolescents, and adults. From 2019 to 2023, she was the Director of the Psychology Department, including the University Counseling Center at the Hellenic American University, and is an Associate Professor of Psychology. She has been an editorial board member and peer reviewer for the *International Journal for Elementary Education* for SciencePG, the *American Journal of Applied Psychology*, and the *International Journal of Progressive Education*. She has published several book chapters and articles and regularly presents her clinical work and research at international conferences in both Europe and the United States. She is a board member of European Branch of American Counseling Association (EB-ACA) and a member of ACA. Sax is a part-time Associate Professor of Psychology at the American College of Greece in the Psychology Department and continues her private practice and consulting as a specialist in her field.

Theodoros Tsirigotis is a clinical psychologist, psychotherapist, and organizational consultant specializing in trauma across hospital, community, NGO, and humanitarian settings. His clinical work integrates psychodynamic, psychoanalytic, and trauma-focused approaches with emphasis on complex trauma, dissociation, and identity fragmentation. He has extensive experience working with refugees, asylum seekers, and survivors of torture, and supports frontline teams exposed to cumulative and secondary trauma. Trained at the Tavistock and Portman NHS Foundation Trust, he works within psychoanalytic and systems-psychodynamic frameworks. He is Director of Education at the European Institute of Counselling and Psychotherapy (EICP) and Head of the Psychological

Center of Chania. He teaches internationally and provides clinical supervision to practitioners working with trauma-exposed populations.

Charitini Zografaki, born and raised in Greece, has always been guided by curiosity, empathy, and imagination. Now living among the vibrant streets of New York, she is a graduate student in Mental Health Counseling at Pace University, bringing over 15 years of experience in caring for others through holistic therapies and healing practices. Her journey has woven together many worlds—psychology, theater, photography, and even the fast-paced rhythm of the banking sector, each adding new colors to her understanding of people and their stories. Fascinated by grief, resilience, and the power of creativity, she believes that every story holds a spark of magic waiting to be found. Fluent in both Greek and English, she draws inspiration from children, nature, and the hidden emotions that live inside us all. When she is not studying or supporting children and families through counseling, you'll find her behind a camera, traveling, or discovering small pieces of everyday magic.

List of Figures

Fig. 1.1	Introduction	3
Fig. 1.2	Maslow's hierarchy of needs (Photo credit: Getty Images/ Stock photos)	4
Fig. 1.3	Baumrind's parenting styles with Maccoby and Martin (Credit: Positive-Parenting-Ally.com)	6
Fig. 1.4	Protecting youth mental health (The U.S. Surgeon General's Advisory, 2021; World Health Organization, 2014; Bronfenbrenner & Ceci, 1994)	15
Fig. 2.1	Dumbo	23
Fig. 3.1	Little Red Riding Hood	35
Fig. 4.1	Pinocchio	47
Fig. 5.1	Hansel and Gretel	57
Fig. 6.1	Peter Pan	69
Fig. 7.1	The Little Mermaid-Ariel	81
Fig. 8.1	Robin Hood	93

CHAPTER 1

Theoretical Introduction

Alessandra Sax

Abstract Childhood and adolescence are both critical periods of lifespan development that encompass necessary aspects of one's environment to foster optimal development—emotionally, socially, cognitively, and physically. What are these important aspects of one's environment? Loved by parents and family members, psychological and physical safety, food, shelter, clothes, and access to education are just a few examples that contribute to healthy development in children and adolescents. All children need these basic needs to thrive optimally at home, in school, and in their communities. When these needs are not met and negative parenting styles are in place, less optimal development and functioning occur. Mental health challenges are on the rise more than ever before with poor parenting and living conditions playing vital roles. Early prevention and outreach programs are needed to support children and adolescents' overall well-being during turbulent times.

Keywords Developmental psychopathology • Adaptive and maladaptive adjustment • Resilience • Parenting styles • Optimal environments • Global mental health • Attachment • Maltreatment • Protective and risk

A. Sax (✉)
The American College of Greece, Athens, Greece
e-mail: asax@acg.edu

A. Sax (ed.), *Understanding Child Psychopathology Through Fairytales*, https://doi.org/10.1007/978-3-032-14097-5_1

factors • Maslow's hierarchy of needs • Diversity of culture • Models of psychopathology • Early prevention

Childhood is a period of development typically ranging from birth to early adolescence (0 months–12 years of age). During the first months and years, infants and children develop bonds with their caregivers in optimal family environments. These optimal environments meet the basic needs of the infant/child (Fig. 1.1). Such needs include love, care, shelter, food, clean clothes, and shoes, as described in Maslow's hierarchy of needs model (1943) (Fig. 1.2).

When an infant and/or child feels safe and protected by their caregiver, healthy development may occur, and developmental milestones can be reached at appropriate stages (i.e., language development, crawling, walking, using eating utensils, and toilet training). Children raised in optimal environments are more likely to develop self-esteem, self-confidence, and thrive academically and socially among their peers. Parenting styles also play an essential role in the developing child's life and are directly correlated with academic success and overall well-being.

Parenting styles have been researched over the last 60 years, particularly in Western society, regarding their role in child development. Studies have indicated that the authoritative parenting style is the most effective in supporting optimal development in children (Febiyanthi & Rachmawati, 2021). However, it is essential to consider how parenting styles around the globe are affected by cultural contexts. Varying cultural values in individualistic or collectivistic cultures shape how one parents and thus one's parenting style. Febiyanthi and Rachmawati (2021) extensively reviewed the literature on parenting practices in the United States, Europe, and Asia to better understand how the best parenting style in one culture may differ from another. Parenting styles are utilized by parents as an approach to introduce culture and the environment to their children.

Baumrind's (1966) theory on parenting styles was one of the most influential theories and informed research on parenting in various countries. Although her research stemmed from the United States and highlighted the authoritative parenting style as the best from the West (Chakkarath, 2010), it is universally applicable to support children in their development and academic progress. Her theory explains three parenting styles, with the fourth style contributed by Maccoby and Martin (1983):

Fig. 1.1 Introduction

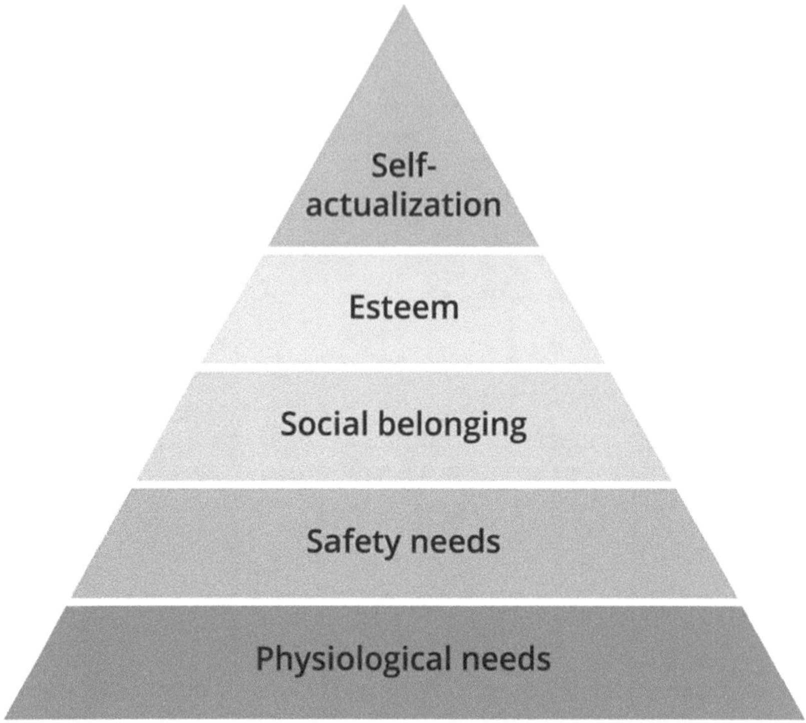

Fig. 1.2 Maslow's hierarchy of needs (Photo credit: Getty Images/Stock photos)

(1) authoritative (mostly applied in Europe and the United States), (2) authoritarian, (3) permissive, and (4) neglectful. She categorized parent's behavior toward their children into two dimensions: (1) parental demandingness and (2) parental responsiveness (Baumrind, 1991). Parental demand refers to the extent that a parent expects and demands their child/children to be mature and responsible. While, parental responsiveness refers to a parent's inclination to provide warmth, support, acceptance, and positive responses toward their child/children's needs (Baumrind, 1989). It is the combination of both parental demandingness and responsiveness that results in the four parenting styles. An authoritarian parent is high on control and low on responsiveness. However, a parent high in control and high in responsiveness fosters an authoritative parenting style. The permissive parent is low in control and high in responsiveness. Lastly,

the parent low in control and responsiveness creates a neglectful parenting style.

Differences in parenting practices are noticeable in the authoritarian parenting style utilized in non-Western cultures. The authoritarian parenting style is perceived as traditional/primitive (Silk et al., 2003). Non-Western parents expect that children are obedient and respectful without receiving resistance from their children, unlike with Western parents. Traditional cultures are generally inclined toward the authoritarian parenting style because they tend to be high in demandingness and responsiveness. Nevertheless, degree of demandingness of authoritarian parents is different from that of authoritative parents from Western countries. Differences in demandingness can be speculated based on the distinctions of each culture (Febiyanti & Rachmawati, 2021).

According to Wishnuwardhani and Mangundjaya (2008), global northern countries entail individualistic cultures, with a focus on the self rather than society, whereas global southern countries hold cultural values that illustrate strong bonds among individuals who are obliged to maintain group loyalty and focus on the community (Wishnuwardhani & Mangundjaya, 2008). Collectivism highly emphasizes the interdependent relationship with one another, while individualism emphasizes self-independency (Triandis, 2001). Kagitcibasi (1970) argued that in collectivist cultures, children perceived controlling parents as being normal and in individualistic cultures, strong control in parents can be interpreted as autocratic and reflects the inhumanity of parents (Kagitcibasi, 1970).

Bornstein (2012) postulated that culture influences parenting, as cultural beliefs and attitudes are maintained and transmitted through generations. Cultural factors such as race, ethnicity, socioeconomic status, education, and religion also influence parenting styles and significantly impact how one parents from one culture to another. What may be considered adaptive in one culture may be considered as maladaptive by another. Therefore, it is essential to bear in mind that the optimal parenting style is highly influenced by the norms and values in the respective culture (Febiyanthi & Rachmawati, 2020) (Fig. 1.3).

Yet, what happens to the infant and/or child who does not have the opportunity to grow up in optimal conditions with optimal parenting? Infants and children who endure any form of small or significant trauma may manifest maladjusted behaviors, which can be either externalized or internalized, depending on the type and severity of the trauma and how

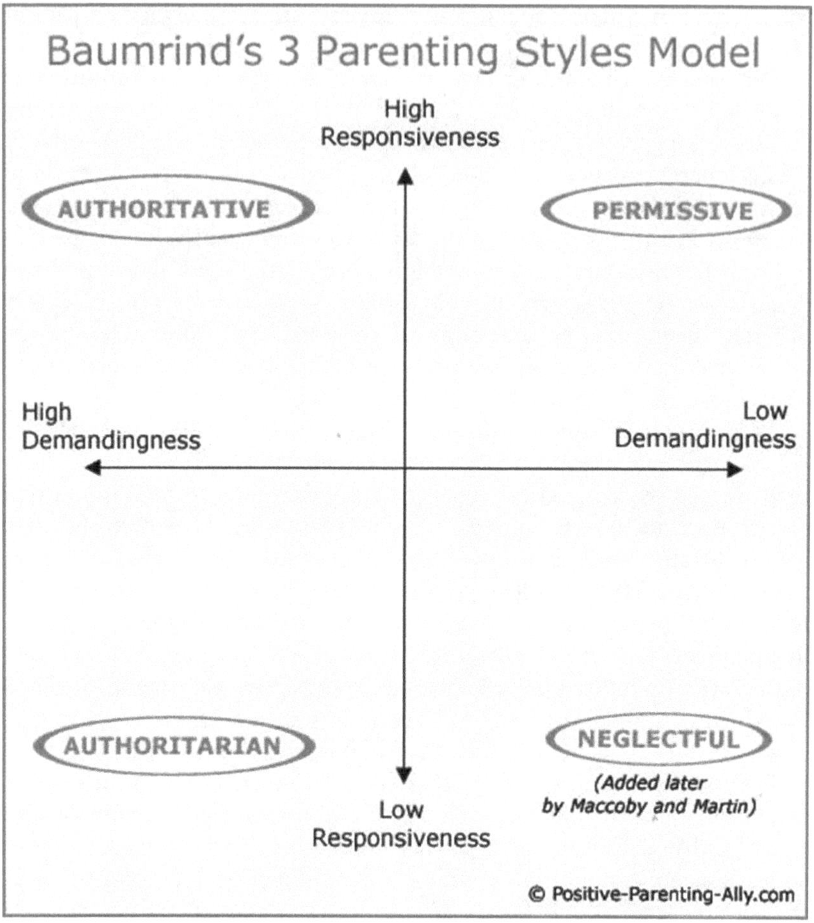

Fig. 1.3 Baumrind's parenting styles with Maccoby and Martin (Credit: Positive-Parenting-Ally.com)

the infant and/or child is able to cope in his/her everyday life. Trauma includes any form of maltreatment, such as emotional, physical, and sexual abuse, as well as neglect.

Data suggests that many children and adolescents who experience physical or sexual abuse display resilience throughout their lives (Perkins & Jones, 2004; Rind et al., 1998). Resilience is an individual's ability to adapt in the face of adversity. Specifically, it refers to the process of capacity for, or outcome of, successful adaptation despite challenging or threatening circumstances (Masten et al., 1990). This resilience, of course, in no way minimizes the moral or legal wrongfulness of maltreatment. Rather, it emphasizes the importance of parents, teachers, and mental health professionals working collaboratively to identify protective factors on individual, familial, and social levels. Resources such as family and peer support, a positive school climate, the presence of nurturing adults, and access to both short- and long-term treatments can foster self-esteem and confidence in children and adolescents (Cicchetti et al., 1997; Perkins & Jones, 2004).

Resilience then reflects the combined contributions of protective factors from individual, family, and societal levels. A child deemed to be resilient in the face of early maltreatment, despite a chaotic and inconsistent home environment, may possess exceptional personal strengths such as an easy temperament, strong intellectual abilities, and a warmth that draws both adults and peers close. Additionally, factors such as the type, duration, and timing of maltreatment also influence resilience. Thus, the construct of resilience can be better understood as the probabilistic outcome of multiple dynamic variables, rather than the static condition of the child or the environment (Yates et al., 2003).

Children who thrive and enjoy advantages in life, such as good health, supportive parents, safe neighborhoods, and effective educational and social systems, are not "resilient"; they are skillful, fortunate, or lucky. In contrast, resilient children do well despite adverse individual, family, or social circumstances. These are the children of adversity who "worked well, played well, loved well, and expected well" (Werner & Smith, 1989).

According to Parritz and Troy (2011), three types of resilient children can be identified: (1) children with many risk factors who achieve good outcomes, (2) children who maintain competence during stressful experiences, and (3) children who display good recoveries following stress or trauma. Developmental psychopathologists have argued that resilience is not a trait or characteristic that certain children have, and others do not. Instead, they see resilience as a process, a capacity that develops over time (Egeland et al., 1993; Freitas & Downey, 1998; Luthar et al., 2000; Masten, 2001; Masten & Reed, 2002). Thus, some children may display certain types of resilience while others do not (i.e., keeping up grades while continuing to struggle emotionally) or resilience that is built up over years (i.e., keeping up grades, mending friendships, and repairing self-image).

Definitions of resilience must also consider positive developmental outcomes. Definitions of abnormality should focus on adequate or optimal adaptations. Additionally, whether good outcomes are simply the absence of clinically significant disorders, or if they encompass the presence of joy and achievements should be considered (Benard, 1999; Cowen et al., 1987; Masten & Reed, 2002).

Connections between the study of resilience and the study of positive psychology are also important (Yates & Masten, 2004). From avoiding legal troubles to achieving award-winning success, acknowledging the range of resilient outcomes through observations should be noted. Keeping these concepts of resilience in mind, descriptions of specific protective factors are critical.

According to Masten et al. (1990), given the presence of risk, protective factors make negative outcomes less likely. It is essential to consider individual, family, and social types of protective factors. The most frequently noted individual factors relate to children's personality characteristics. Children who have sunny dispositions, engaging manners, and higher intelligence tend to fare better. Family factors, such as family cohesion and warmth, play a crucial role as well. Having supportive, emotionally available, and dedicated parents makes it more likely that at-risk children can avoid an ever-increasing string of negative events than children with less capable parents.

Recent research on children living in poverty suggests that resilience is not uncommon and is associated with both genetic and environmental factors (Buckner et al., 2003; Kim-Cohen et al., 2004). Social factors play a role as well (Garmezy, 1985; Rickel & Becker, 1997). Children embedded in ethnic, cultural, or religious communities where their well-being is a communal responsibility may have access to support and resources that are unavailable to others. From both theoretical and clinical perspectives, at-risk children with access to economic and political advantages, such as psychological counseling or school-based services, have better outcomes.

To appreciate the complexities of patterns of protection, looking at children in the same family who face similar risks may develop different outcomes. The factors that promote better outcomes given specific psychopathologies need to be examined carefully (Kilmer et al., 2001). How do these protective factors exert their beneficial effects? What are the mechanisms by which they influence the course and direction of children's developmental pathways? Rutter (1987, 1990) suggests that protective factors influence children's outcomes by: (1) decreasing the impact of risk, (2) reducing the negative chain reactions that follow exposure to risk, (3) serving to establish or maintain self-esteem and self-efficacy, and (4) opening up opportunities for improvement and/or growth.

Reducing the impact of risk involves minimizing children's exposure to negative events. It may also involve changing how they perceive exposure, so that they view risk factors in less harmful ways. For example, a child who has experienced physical or sexual abuse can be encouraged to see themselves as heroics for reporting the abuse, thus protecting other sufferers. Reducing negative chain reactions involves intervening before a series of negative responses or additional negative events occur. For example, a child who experiences separation anxiety and misses school may be quickly referred for therapy with a plan put into place to help the child return to the classroom. This approach prevents reinforcing the behavior of staying at home to avoid anxiety, thereby avoiding academic difficulties resulting from missed class assignments. Support from family members or friends can also help children before they become overwhelmed by frustration or panic.

Developing and maintaining self-esteem and self-efficacy is clearly related to our understanding of the role of personality characteristics in moderating distress and dysfunction. For example, a student with dyslexia who is given the opportunity to meet other students with dyslexia is less likely to view processing new information as evidence of personal inferiority, lack of intelligence, or insufficient effort. Lastly, Rutter (1987, 1990) indicated that protective factors influence children's outcomes, opening opportunities for improvement and growth, and involves the appreciation of turning points in children's lives. Recognizing the developmental challenges that children face when taking advantage of both the expected and unexpected bumps in their road of development may have noticeable effects. For a straightforward example, we can consider that a move to a new neighborhood may help a child form new friendships, despite the change. In a more paradoxical example, Parmelee (1986) discussed the beneficial effects of illnesses in children, as minor illnesses such as a virus or a broken bone allow children to experience small frustrations that help to develop coping efforts. Such experiences allow children to successfully cope with more serious or difficult stressors later in life. A child who never experiences frustration or disappointment is thus at a disadvantage, as he or she can easily become upset and without well-practiced strategies when inevitable stress occurs. The possible relations between the experience of stress and the capacity to cope are complex, yet very necessary for child development.

Understanding psychopathology is complex. Parents, teachers, and children themselves are often confused about whether a particular pattern of feelings, thoughts, and behaviors reflects an actual disorder, and if so, whether that disorder involves minor, moderate, or major maladjustment. One of the first steps leading to accurate and useful conceptualizations of psychopathology is to recognize the many connections between "normal" and "abnormal" development. It is important to consider other children's normal experiences of wariness and fear, differences among children's temperaments, and how distress may interfere with daily life. Models of childhood and child development have been influenced by changing historical notions of children being as being seen as miniature adults, blank slates, savages, and innocent beings; as well more recent of children being seen as innately and surprisingly competent individuals (Elkind, 1994; Hwang et al., 1996; Mintz, 2006; White, 1996). Depending on the model, our understanding of childhood may lead us to expect that almost all normally developing children will engage in idyllic play, skill learning and practice, and avoid danger. Whether most children can amuse themselves for hours on end, practice piano, or take swimming lessons without complaining, or never run into the street without looking for cars should realistically be evaluated as "normal"/adaptive. Hence, it is the intensity and frequency with which these behaviors occur that can be assessed as "abnormal"/maladaptive.

Most contemporary theorists, researchers, and clinicians emphasize that a useful model of normal development demands a dynamic appreciation of children's strengths and weaknesses, advances and setbacks, and resolved challenges alongside new ones. A model like this accounts for the complexities of individual, familial, ethnic, cultural, and societal beliefs regarding desirable and undesirable outcomes for children and adolescents. Against this multilayered background of normal child development are those children whose identifiable distress and dysfunction are exceptional. Empirically sound and clinically appropriate definitions of disorder can be provided only if various beliefs, along with data, about what constitutes normal behavior are carefully examined (Parritz & Troy, 2011). Mentally healthy children and adolescents should experience and enjoy a positive quality of life. They should function well at home, in school, and in their communities, both intrapersonally and interpersonally. Children and adolescents who experience a negative quality of life, poor functioning at home, school, and in communities, may be at higher risk of developing mental health conditions.

Therefore, what is considered normal? Common descriptions of normality and psychopathology often focus on three aspects: (1) statistical deviance, which considers the infrequency of certain emotions, cognitions, and/or behaviors; (2) sociocultural norms, which relate to the beliefs and expectations of certain groups regarding what kinds of emotions, cognitions, and/or behaviors are undesirable or unacceptable; and (3) mental health definitions, which encompass theoretical or clinically based notions of distress and dysfunction (Parritz & Troy, 2011).

From a statistical deviance perspective, a child who displays too much or too little of any age-expected behavior (such as dependency or assertiveness) may be considered to have a disorder. Children of a certain age above the "high number" cutoff, or below the "low number" cutoff, would meet the criterion for a disorder (Parritz & Troy, 2011). From a sociocultural norm perspective, children who fail to conform to expectations they adopt as age- or gender-specific beliefs about themselves, or who express discomfort with displaying expected age- or gender-based behaviors, might have a disorder (Parritz & Troy, 2011). Pressure in a particular neighborhood or peer group to adopt belligerent or aggressive behavior, for instance, may contribute to the diagnosis of psychopathology by outsiders. Depending on the particular social and cultural settings, norms will vary, but there will always be certain patterns of emotion, cognition, and behavior that are considered evidence of psychopathology (Parritz & Troy, 2011).

The role of values in these definitions also warrants further examination, as each definition raises questions about the influence of values in conceptualizing mental health and psychopathology. Regardless of whether definitions of psychopathology and disorders focus on statistical deviance, sociocultural norms, or mental health evaluations, they all require several types of value judgments (Sonuga-Barke, 1988; Wakefield, 2002). One important value judgment involves personal or group standards of adequate or average adaptation, or optimal adaptation (Offer, 1999). Adequate adaptation refers to what is considered acceptable or good enough, while optimal adaptation has to do with what is excellent, superior, or the best possible outcome. Definitions of psychopathology describe intense, frequent, and/or persistent maladaptive patterns of emotion, cognition, and behavior. Developmental psychopathology extends this description to emphasize that these maladaptive patterns occur in the context of normal development and result in the current and potential impairment of infants, children, and adolescents (Parritz & Troy, 2011).

The multipart task of estimating rates of disorder includes: (1) identifying children with clinically significant distress and dysfunction, whether or not they are in treatment, (2) calculating the levels of general and specific psychopathologies, along with the impairments associated with various disorders, and (3) tracking changing trends in the identification and diagnosis of specific categories of disorder (i.e., autism, attention deficit hyperactivity disorder, and depression) (Maughan et al., 2005; Prosser & McArdle, 1996; Roberts et al., 1998; Rutter & Smith, 1995).

The prevalence of disorders in infants, children, and adolescents can be estimated using varied methodologies and within varied groups (Bird, 1996; Hackett & Hackett, 1999; Lahey et al., 1996; Roberts et al., 1998). Prevalence and incidence rates are both measures of psychopathology cases in a population. Prevalence refers to all current cases; incidence refers to new cases in any given time. One method for estimating prevalence is random sampling of a general population through surveys, phone questionnaires, and/or detailed psychopathology screening instruments. Another approach involves sampling in schools using teachers' assessments. Samples can also focus on the types of disorders seen in children's primary care and mental health clinics. Whichever method is selected, there can be no doubt that many children struggle with clinically significant disorders.

UNCIF (2024) has estimated that roughly 11.2 million (13%) of children and young people, 19 years old and younger in the European Union, suffer from a mental health condition (Global Burden of Disease Study, 2021). Rates increase with age from nearly 2% of children under the age of 5 to around 19% of youth, 15 to 19 years old. In total, 5.9 million males and 5.3 million females up to the age of 19 have mental health conditions. Rates are higher for males than for females up to the age of 14 and slightly higher for females than for males aged 15–19 years old. Among those aged 15 to 19, approximately 8% suffer from anxiety and 4% from depression. Rates for both conditions are higher in females for this age group (9.6% and 4.6%) than in males (5.5% and 2.6%) (Global Burden of Disease Study, 2021). Research suggests that mental health problems among European youth increased during the COVID-19 pandemic (Wolf &

Schmitz, 2023). The longer-term impact of the pandemic on child and adolescent mental health is still unspecified (UNICEF, 2024).

Challenges with mental health were the leading cause of disability and poor life outcomes in young people even before the COVID-19 pandemic, with up to 1 in 5 children ages 3 to 17 in the United States reporting a mental, emotional, developmental, or behavioral disorder (Perou et al., 2013).

In the US Surgeon General's Report (2021), 21% of children between the ages of 9 and 17 met diagnostic criteria for a disorder associated with at least minimum impairment, 11% met diagnostic criteria for disorders associated with significant impairment, and 5% met the diagnostic criteria for disorders associated with extreme impairment (Surgeon General's Report, 2001). In 2016, of the 7.7 million children with treatable mental health disorders, almost half of them did not receive adequate treatment (Whitney & Peterson, 2019).

Unfortunately, in recent years, national surveys of youth have shown major increases in certain mental health symptoms, including depressive symptoms and suicidal ideation. From 2009 to 2019, the proportion of high school students reporting persistent feelings of sadness or hopelessness increased by 40%; the share seriously considering attempting suicide increased by 36%; and the share creating a suicide plan increased by 44% (Centers for Disease Control and Prevention, 2020). During the years 2011 and 2015, youth psychiatric visits to emergency wards for depression, anxiety, and behavioral challenges increased by 28% (Kalb et al., 2019). Between 2007 and 2018, suicide rates among youth ages 10–24 in the United States increased by 57% (Curtin, 2020). Early estimates from the National Center for Health Statistics suggested more than 6600 deaths by suicide occurred among individuals between 10 and 24 years of age in 2020 (Curtin et al., 2021).

More recently, globally, the World Health Organization estimated that one in seven (14%) of 10–19-year-olds experiences mental health conditions (World Health Organization Report, 2024). Anxiety disorders (which may involve panic or excessive worry) are the most prevalent in this age group and are more common among older adolescents. It is estimated that 4.4% of 10–14-year-olds and 5.5% of 15–19-year-olds experience an anxiety disorder (World Health Organization Report, 2024). Depression is estimated to occur among 1.4% of youth 10–14 years of age and 3.5% of 15–19-year-olds (World Health Organization Report, 2024).

Worldwide, 8% of children and 15% of adolescents experience a mental disorder. However, most of these youth did not seek help or receive care, with suicide being the third leading cause of death in 15–29-year-olds (World Health Organization Report, 2024). Children and adolescents with mental health challenges are more vulnerable to social exclusion, discrimination, stigma (affecting readiness to seek help), educational difficulties, risk-taking behaviors, health problems, and violations of their human rights (World Health Organization Report, 2024).

Various theoretical models (i.e., psychodynamic, physiological, behavioral, cognitive, family systems, etc.) of development, psychopathology, and treatment help to organize clinical observations, direct research efforts, and design treatment programs when providing mental services to children and adolescents. More specifically, when working with children and adolescents, continuous models of psychopathology emphasize the gradual transition from the normal range of emotions, thoughts, and behaviors to clinically significant problems, whereas discontinuous models focus on the differences between distinct patterns of emotion, cognition, and behavior within the normal range and those that define clinical disorders.

However, regardless of the specific model adhered to in the development and course of treatment, sociocultural models or diversity of culture models highlight the importance of the social context, including gender, sexual orientation, race, ethnicity, socioeconomic status, language, religion, disability, education, occupation, and more (Parritz & Troy, 2011). Preventive and outreach programs and policies must be considered and implemented globally. UNICEF's (2024) policy on Child and Adolescent Mental Health in the European Union has addressed the following needs to support children and adolescent mental health and overall well-being: (1) a comprehensive, multi-sectoral Mental Health Strategy from the European Commission, based on socio-ecological, inclusive, and human rights approaches, (2) improved evidence-based data collection, (3) increased EU funds for actions on mental health, with a focus on prevention, early intervention, and quality, age-appropriate, community-based mental health services, (4) free access to quality health services of the European Child Guarantee, including children with mental health conditions, (5) mainstreaming mental health in all EU policies—both internal and external. This would ensure that mental health considerations are built into the design, implementation, monitoring, and evaluation of policy, legislation, and spending programs, and (6) raising awareness and intercepting stigma with an EU initiative (UNICEF, 2024).

Both childhood and adolescence are critical life stages for mental health. These developmental stages are a time when there is rapid growth and development of the brain. Cognitive and social-emotional skills shape the future mental health of children and adolescents and are important for assuming adult roles in society. The quality of the environment in which children and adolescents are raised shapes their well-being and development. Early negative experiences at home, school, or in digital spaces, such as exposure to violence, bullying, poverty, or the mental illness of a parent or other caregiver, all increase the risk of mental illness. The consequences of not addressing mental health and psychosocial development for children and adolescents extend into adulthood and limit opportunities for leading fulfilling lives that they greatly deserve (World Health Organization Report, 2024) (Fig. 1.4).

Fig. 1.4 Protecting youth mental health (The U.S. Surgeon General's Advisory, 2021; World Health Organization, 2014; Bronfenbrenner & Ceci, 1994)

References

Baumrind, D. (1991). The influence of parenting style on adolescent competence and substance use. *The Journal of Early Adolescence, 11*(1), 56–95. https://doi.org/10.1177/0272431691111004

Baumrind, D. (1989). Rearing competent children. In W. Damon (Ed.), *The Jossey-Bass social and behavioural science series, child development today and tomorrow* (pp. 349–378). San Francisco Jossey-Bass.

Baumrind, D. (1966). Effects of authoritative parental control on child behavior. *Child Development, 37*(4), 887–907.

Benard, B. (1999). Applications of resilience: Possibilities and promise. In M. D. Glantz & J. L. Johnson (Eds.), *Resilience and development: Positive life adaptations. Longitudinal research in the social and behavioral sciences* (pp. 269–277). Kluwer Academic Publishers.

Bird, H. R. (1996). Epidemiology of childhood disorders in a cross-cultural context. *Journal of Child Psychology and Psychiatry, 37*(1), 35–49.

Bornstein, M. H. (2012). Cultural approaches to parenting. *Parenting, 12*(3), 212–221. https://doi.org/10.1080/15295192.2012.683359

Bronfenbrenner, U., & Ceci, S. J. (1994). Nature-nurture reconceptualized in developmental perspective: A bioecological model. *Psychological Review, 101*(4), 568–586. https://doi.org/10.1037/0033-295X.101.4.568

Buckner, J. C., Mezzacappa, E., & Beardslee, W. R. (2003). Characteristics of resilient youths living in poverty: The role of self-regulatory processes. *Development and Psychopathology, 15*, 139–162.

Centers for Disease Control and Prevention. (2020). Youth behavior surveillance data summary & trends report: 2009–2019. https://www.cdc.gov/nchhstp/dear_colleague/2020/dcl-102320-YRBS-2009-2019-report.html

Chakkarath, P. (2010). Stereotypes in social psychology: The "west-east" differentiation as a reflection of western traditions of thought. *Psychological Studies, 55*(1), 18–25.

Cicchetti, D., Rogosch, F. A., & Toth, S. L. (1997). Ontogenesis, depressotypic organization, and the depressive spectrum. In S. Luthar, J. Burack, D. Cicchetti, & J. R. Weisz (Eds.), *Developmental psychopathology: Perspectives on adjustment, risk and disorder* (pp. 273–313). Cambridge University Press.

Cowen, E. L., Work, W. C., & Wyman, P. A. (1987). The Rochester child resilience project (RCRP): Facts found, lessons learned, future directions divined. In S. S. Luthar & J. E. Burack (Eds.), *Developmental psychopathology: Perspectives on adjustment, risk, and disorder* (pp. 527–547). Cambridge University Press.

Curtin, S. C. (2020). *State suicide rates among adolescents and young adults aged 10–24: United States, 2000–2018* (National Vital Statistics Reports; Vol. 69, no. 11). National Center for Health Statistics.

Curtin, S. C., Hedegaard, H., & Ahmad, F. B. (2021). *Provisional numbers and rates of suicide by month and demographic characteristics: United States, 2020* (Vital Statistics Rapid Release; 16). National Center for Health Statistics.

Egeland, B., Carlson, E., & Sroufe, L. A. (1993). Resilience as process. *Development and Psychopathology, 5*, 517–528.
Elkind, D. (1994). *Ties that stress.* Harvard University Press.
Febiyanti, A., Rachmawati, Y. (2021). Is Authoritative Parenting the Best Parenting Style?. https://doi.org/10.2991/assehr.k.210322.021
Freitas, A. L., & Downey, G. (1998). Resilience: A dynamic perspective. *International Journal of Behavioral Development, 22*(2), 263–285.
Garmezy, N. (1985). The NIMH-Israeli high-risk study: Commendation, comments, and cautions. *Schizophrenia Bulletin, 11*(3), 349–354.
Global Burden of Disease Study (2021). Retrieved August 6, 2025, from https://vizhub.healthdata.org/gbd-results/
Hackett, R., & Hackett, L. (1999). Child psychiatry across cultures. *International Review of Psychiatry, 11*, 225–235.
Hwang, C. P., Lamb, M. E., & Sigel, I. E. (1996). *Images of childhood.* Erlbaum.
Kalb, L. G., Stapp, E. K., Ballard, E. D., Holingue, C., Keefer, A., & Riley, A. (2019). Trends in psychiatric emergency department visits among youth and young adults in the US. *Pediatrics, 143*(4). https://doi.org/10.1542/peds.2018-2192
Kagitcibasi, C. (1970). Social norms and authoritarianism: A Turkish-American comparison. *Journal of Personality and Social Psychology, 16*(3), 444–451. https://psycnet.apa.org/record/1971-04049-001
Kilmer, R. P., Cowen, E. L., & Wyman, P. A. (2001). A microlevel analysis of developmental, parenting, and family milieu variables that differentiate stress-resilient and stress-affected children. *Journal of Community Psychology, 29*(4), 391–416.
Kim-Cohen, J., Moffitt, T. E., Caspi, A., & Taylor, A. (2004). Genetic and environmental processes in young children's resilience and vulnerability to socioeconomic deprivation. *Child Development, 75*, 651–668.
Lahey, B. B., Flagg, E. W., Bird, H. R., Schwab-Stone, M. E., Canino, G., Dulcan, M. K., Leaf, P. J., Davies, M., Brogan, D., Bourdon, K., Horwitz, S. M., Rubio-Stipec, M., Freeman, D. H., Lichtman, J. H., Shaffer, D., Goodman, S. H., Narrow, W. E., Weissman, M. M., Kandel, D. B., Jensen, P. S., Richters, J. E., & Regier, D. A. (1996). The NIMH methods for the epidemiology of child and adolescent mental disorders (MECA) study: Background and methodology. *Journal of the American Academy of Child and Adolescent Psychiatry, 35*(7), 855–865.
Luthar, S. S., Cicchetti, D., & Becker, B. (2000). Research on resilience: Response to commentaries. *Child Development, 71*(3), 573–575.
Maccoby, E. E., & Martin, J. A. (1983). Socialization in the context of the family: Parent-child interaction. *Handbook of Child Psychology, 4*, 1–102.
Maslow, A. H. (1943). A theory of human motivation. *Psychological Review, 50*(4), 430–437.

Masten, A. S. (2001). Ordinary magic: Resilience processes in development. *American Psychologist, 56*(3), 227–238.
Masten, A. S., Best, K. M., & Garmezy, N. (1990). Resilience and development: Contributions from the study of children who overcome adversity. *Development and Psychopathology, 2*, 425–444.
Masten, A. S., Morison, P., Pellegrini, D., & Tellegen, A. (1990). Competence under stress: Risk and protective factors. In J. E. Rolf & A. S. Masten (Eds.), *Risk and protective factors in the development of psychopathology* (pp. 236–256). Cambridge University Press.
Masten, A. S., & Reed, M.-G. J. (2002). Resilience in development. In C. R. Snyder & S. J. Lopez (Eds.), *Handbook of positive psychology* (pp. 74–88). Oxford University Press.
Maughan, B., Iervolino, A. C., & Collishaw, S. (2005). Time trends in child and adolescent mental disorders. *Current Opinion on Psychiatry, 18*(4), 381–385.
Mintz, S. (2006). *Huck's raft: A history of American childhood*. Belknap Press.
Offer, D. (1999). Normality and the boundaries of psychiatry. In S. Weissman & M. Sabshin (Eds.), *Psychiatry in the new millennium* (pp. 67–77). American Psychiatric Association.
Parmelee, A. H. (1986). Children's illnesses: Their beneficial effects on behavioral development. *Child Development, 57*(1), 1–10. https://doi.org/10.2307/1130632
Perkins, D. F., & Jones, K. R. (2004). Risk behaviors and resiliency within physically abused adolescents. *Child Abuse and Neglect, 28*, 547–563.
Perou, R., Bitsko, R. H., Blumberg, S. J., Pastor, P., Ghandour, R. M., Gfroerer, J. C., Hedden, S. L., Crosby, A. E., Visser, S. N., Schieve, L. A., Parks, S. E., Hall, J. E., Brody, D., Simile, C. M., Thompson, W. W., Baio, J., Avenevoli, S., Kogan, M. D., Huang, L. N., & Centers for Disease Control and Prevention (CDC). (2013). Mental health surveillance among children—United States, 2005-2011. *MMWR. Morbidity and Mortality Weekly Report Supplements, 62*(2), 1–35.
Prosser, J., & McArdle, P. (1996). The changing mental health of children and adolescents: Evidence for deterioration? *Psychological Medicine, 26*(4), 715–725.
Rickel, A. U., & Becker, E. (1997). Risk factors in infancy and early childhood. In A. U. Rickel & E. Becker (Eds.), *Keeping children from harm's way: How national policy affects psychological development* (pp. 27–57). American Psychological Association.
Rind, B., Tromovich, P., & Bauserman, R. (1998). A meta-analytic examination of assumed properties of child sexual abuse using college samples. *Psychological Bulletin, 124*, 22–53.
Roberts, R. E., Attkisson, C. C., & Rosenblatt, A. (1998). Prevalence of psychopathology among children and adolescents. *American Journal of Psychiatry, 155*(6), 715–725.

Rutter, M. (1987). Psychosocial resilience and protective mechanisms. *American Journal of Orthopsychiatry, 57*(3), 316–331.
Rutter, M. (1990). Psychosocial resilience and protective mechanisms. In J. E. Rolf & A. S. Masten (Eds.), *Risk and protective factors in the development of psychopathology* (pp. 181–214). Cambridge University Press.
Rutter, M., & Smith, D. J. (1995). *Psychological disorders in young people: Time trends and their causes.* Wiley.
Silk, J. S., Steinberg, L., & Morris, A. S. (2003). Adolescents' emotion regulation in daily life: Links to depressive symptoms and problem behaviour. *Child Development, 74*(6), 1869–1880.
Sonuga-Barke, E. J. S. (1988). Categorical models of childhood disorder: A conceptual and empirical analysis. *Journal of Child Psychology and Psychiatry, 39*(1), 115–133.
The U.S. Surgeon General's Advisory. (2021, December 6). *Protecting youth mental health,* 1–53.
Triandis, H. C. (2001). Individualism-collectivism and personality. *Journal of Personality, 69*(6), 907–924. https://doi.org/10.1111/1467-6494.696169
UNICEF for Every Child, Policy Brief 2. (2024). *Child and adolescent mental health: The state of children in the European Union.*
Wakefield, J. C. (2002). Values and the validity of diagnostic criteria: Disvalued versus disordered conditions of childhood and adolescence. In J. Z. Sadler (Ed.), *Descriptions and prescriptions: Values, mental disorders and the DSMs* (pp. 148–164). Johns Hopkins University Press.
Werner, E. E., & Smith, R. S. (1989). *Vulnerable but invincible: A study of resilient children.* McGraw-Hill.
White, S. H. (1996). Developmental psychopathology: From attribution toward information. In S. Matthysse & D. L. Levy (Eds.), *Psychopathology: The evolving science of mental disorder* (pp. 161–197). Cambridge University Press.
Whitney, D. G., & Peterson, M. (2019). US national and state-level prevalence of mental health disorders and disparities of mental health care use in children. *JAMA Pediatrics, 173*(4), 389–391. https://doi.org/10.1001/jamapediatrics.2018.5399
Wishnuwardhani, P. D., & Mangundjaya, W. (2008). Hubungan nilai budayaindividualisme-kolektivisme dan gaya penyelesaian konflik. *Jurnal Psikologi Sosial, 14*(1), 5–8.
Wolf, K., & Schmitz, J. (2023). Scoping review: Longitudinal effects of the COVID-19 pandemic on child and adolescent mental health. *European Child & Adolescent Psychiatry.* https://doi.org/10.1007/s00787-023-02206-8
World Health Organization Report. (2024, October 10).
World Health Organization. (2014). *Health for the world's adolescents: A second chance in the second decade.* WHO Press, World Health Organization. https://

apps.who.int/adolescent/second-decade/files/1612_MNCAH_HWA_Executive_Summary.pdf

Yates, T. M., Egeland, B., & Sroufe, L. A. (2003). Rethinking resilience: A developmental process perspective. In S. S. Luthar (Ed.), *Resilience and vulnerability: Adaptation in the context of childhood adversities* (pp. 243–266). Cambridge University Press.

Yates, T. M., & Masten, A. S. (2004). Fostering the future: Resilience theory and the practice of positive psychology. In P. A. Linsley & S. Joseph (Eds.), *Positive psychology in practice* (pp. 521–539). Wiley.

CHAPTER 2

Dumbo the Elephant

Anna Rombotis

Abstract This chapter explores the character Dumbo, the flying elephant delivered to his mother by a stork, from the 1941 Disney film. In human years, he would be between two and four years of age, in elephant years, five to ten years. Dumbo is separated from his mother due to discriminatory behavior toward him for his big ears. Dumbo witnesses his mother being maltreated by the circus owner where they both live. After this disturbing event, Dumbo realizes he can fly as he is found in a tree, inebriated over what happened to his mother. His unique development will be assessed and diagnosed while taking into consideration his emotional, social, physical, and cognitive development. In this vignette, Dumbo is diagnosed with intellectual developmental disorder and is assessed through evaluating his demographics, risk factors, protective factors, attachment style, etiology of the syndrome/disorder, and clinical treatment interventions.

Keywords Early childhood • Risk factors • Protective factors • Attachment style • Discrimination • Intellectual developmental disorder

A. Rombotis (✉)
Hellenic American University Alumna, Athens, Greece
e-mail: arombotis@hauniv.edu

A. Sax (ed.), *Understanding Child Psychopathology Through Fairytales*, https://doi.org/10.1007/978-3-032-14097-5_2

The Story of Dumbo

The old Disney film, Dumbo (1941), is the story of a unique young elephant named Dumbo. Dumbo was delivered by a stork to his mother, Ms. Jumbo, who lives as a circus elephant in Florida, United States. As his mother unravels him from the blanket he was carried in, an immediate strong bond is formed. However, the other elephants soon discover that Dumbo is very different from them, as he has extraordinarily large ears. As a result, the female elephants begin to make nasty remarks, stating, "His ears are funny". Further, when his mother tries to name him Jumbo Jr., she is ridiculed by the other elephants and told, "you mean, Dumbo!", which is how he got his name (Fig. 2.1).

Ms. Jumbo does not care for their comments and instead focuses only on providing the right care for her newborn. However, an incident occurs, causing her and Dumbo to be separated from each other. Some kids tease Dumbo for his ears, and as a result, his mother tries to fight back and protect him, which leads the circus men to bind her in chains and separate her from him. The scene is violent and scary, as Dumbo witnesses his mother being whipped, bound in chains, and placed in solitary confinement. Consequently, the female elephants call him a freak, "a disgrace", ignore him, and seclude him from their group. At this point, Dumbo befriends a mouse who helps him get a role in the elephant pyramid skit. However, upon his cue in the skit, he trips, causing the pyramid to collapse. He is then appointed to play a clown, in which role he appears greatly unhappy and dissatisfied. The clowns want to take advantage of him and raise the platform he must jump from. He is portrayed as though he has no feelings. After a brief encounter with his mother behind bars, he accidentally drinks a barrel full of alcohol with his mouse friend, gets drunk, and wakes up in a tree. A group of crows discovers that Dumbo was able to fly up the tree with his ears when he was drunk. This leads to him becoming a huge circus star, with his name in the newspapers. His uniqueness and flying ability lead him to gain respect from the other elephants, after which his mother is finally released from solitary, and they are happily reunited.

Demographic Background

Dumbo has a very interesting background, through which one can draw many conclusions. From the film, it can be deduced that he was probably adopted, given that he was delivered to his mother by a stork. Moreover,

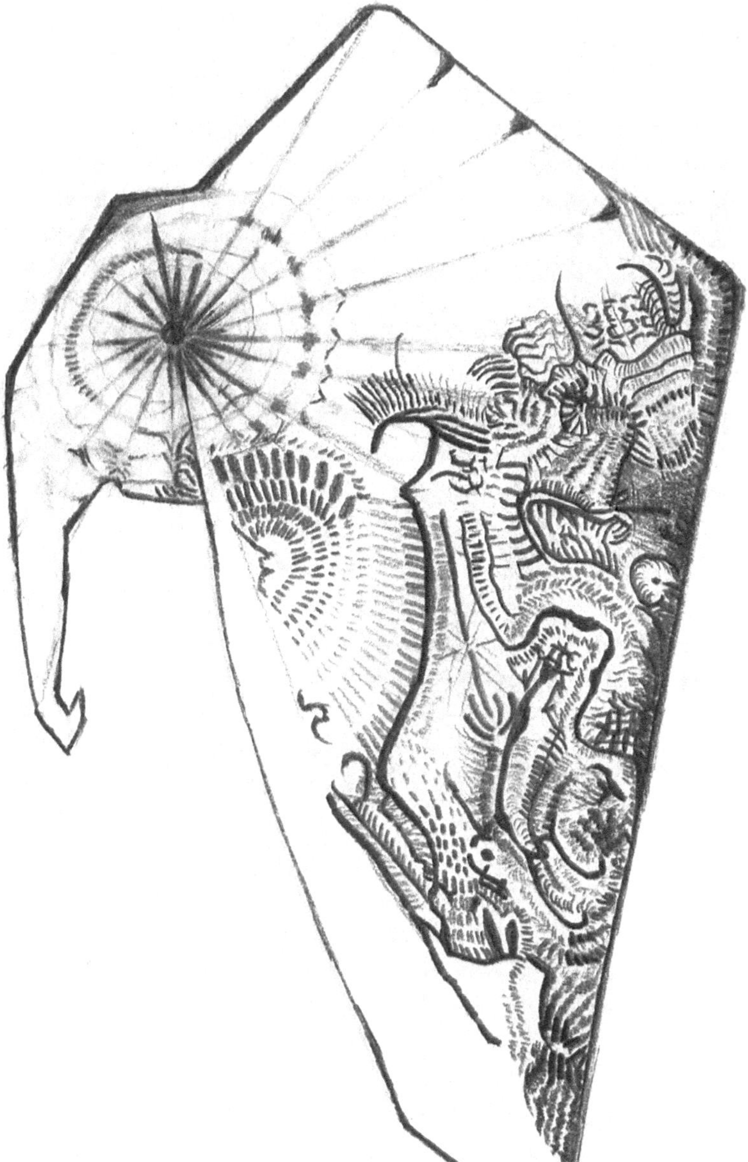

Fig. 2.1 Dumbo

it is evident that Dumbo does not have a father. Furthermore, his mouse friend even refers to him as an orphan at the end (although this could have also been said in the context that his mother is unable to care for him while she was confined). With regards to his age, it can be deduced that he is only a calf (i.e., a baby elephant), probably a few months or years old. It is difficult to give an exact age here because baby elephants are dependent on their mothers for milk, which can last from five to ten years (Meyer, 2015). However, in human years, it can be speculated that he would be between two and four years old. This is because of his apparent ability to understand spoken words; furthermore, his gross motor skills are quite good. Elephants are only indigenous to Africa and Asia (Shoshani, 2020); therefore, it can be theorized that the elephants were all imported from abroad and perhaps Dumbo was delivered by the stork from across the Atlantic.

Psychodynamic Analysis

The following analysis covers the social, physical, cognitive, and emotional domains of Dumbo's background. His social history is quite upsetting, given that he was labeled an outcast, a "freak", by the herd very early on in his life. He was even ridiculed by the human boys and had no friends other than a kind mouse. He was also forced to play the part of a clown, causing him evident distress and leading to low self-confidence. His physical make-up is unknown, except for his apparent large ears. This abnormality is what gives him the ability to fly, which is unheard of among elephants. Next, concerning his cognitive abilities, it is apparent that Dumbo can understand most of what is being said to him, but he does not communicate verbally. This could be because he is too young; however, his mother also possesses the same trait, unlike the other elephants. Further (removed "to this"), Dumbo was unable to understand some instances when he was being made fun of, suggesting that he is quite innocent and naïve. Additionally, it can be hypothesized that Dumbo is in Erikson's Autonomy versus Doubt stage (1963, as cited in Boyd & Bee, 2019), whereby he is experiencing shame and doubt with regard to his abnormally large ears. This stage is overcome when he chooses to embrace his uniqueness and turn it into a gift, providing himself with a sense of self--control and adequacy, which can be seen at the resolution of the film. Finally, Dumbo is very in tune with his emotions, whereby he is not afraid to show his excitement or love toward his mouse friend and especially his mother. Moreover, he expresses his sadness outwardly by crying and shrugging his shoulders. It appears Dumbo can pick up on emotional cues, suggesting that he has a high emotional intelligence (Boyd & Bee, 2019).

Risk Factors

Dumbo has been unfortunate to have experienced many risk factors. Starting chronologically, he was delivered on a rainy night, perhaps causing him some feelings of fear and trauma. Additionally, if it is assumed that he was adopted, this could also pose a risk factor regarding the importance of creating a secure bond with the primary caregiver during the early years. Furthermore, from the start, it was apparent that he was born with abnormally large ears. This caused him to be a victim of bullying and much ridicule from others and his own herd. As a result of his mother's attempts to protect him, he was forcibly separated from her in a violent manner, causing him to witness her being bound, whipped, chained, and placed in solitary confinement, and labeled as a "crazy elephant". Moreover, the bullying also led him to be secluded from the other elephants, preventing him from socializing with others his age, which is important for his development. Another risk factor was that he was forced to play a clown in the circus rather than join the other elephants. This could have led him to feel depersonalized regarding his own identity as an elephant and to experience people laughing at him again.

Protective Factors

Despite the many risk factors, Dumbo does possess some protective factors (Parritz & Troy, 2011). Most importantly, he created a strong attachment to his mother who is evidently nurturing, loving, and protective of him. When his mother was taken from him, he was lucky enough to befriend a kind and boisterous mouse who made him feel accepted and increased his self-esteem. Another protective factor was the encouraging crows that he met toward the end of the film. Although they appeared to tease him at first, they were the ones to suggest that he could fly and gave him the courage to do so with their gift, a "magic feather".

Attachment Style

It is evident that Dumbo has created a secure attachment with his mother from the first time they met. His mother immediately accepted him for who he was and cradled him in her arms. She would bathe him (removed "as well") and protect him from external threats. When she was no longer physically able to do so, she would still extend her trunk to caress and cradle him from outside (removed "of") her confined cage. Furthermore, when separated from his mother, Dumbo showed evident distress, as did his mother. All these instances characterize their attachment as secure in accordance with Ainsworth's theory (as cited in Boyd & Bee, 2019). Ainsworth emphasizes that a secure attachment is based on the child's and mother's ability to separate with some distress but then adapt (as cited in Boyd & Bee, 2019). When in need, the child will try to seek out their mother and will be happy to see her when reunited. The mother is quite sensitive, consistent, and attuned to her child's needs, allowing her child to feel a sense of trust and security.

Diagnosis and Assessment

For Dumbo's case, it seems as though he could be diagnosed with an intellectual developmental disability (IDD). IDD is a neurodevelopmental condition characterized by significant limitations in both intellectual functioning—such as reasoning, problem-solving, and learning—and adaptive behavior, which encompasses conceptual, social, and practical skills (American Association on Intellectual and Developmental Disabilities [AAIDD], 2025a). IDD originates during the developmental period, typically before the age of 18, and results from various causes, including genetic conditions, prenatal or perinatal complications, brain injury, or environmental factors (Hazarika et al., 2017; Saad & ElAdl, 2019). The condition varies in severity, requiring different levels of support across the lifespan, and is diagnosed through standardized assessments of cognitive ability and adaptive functioning, following established diagnostic criteria such as those in the DSM-5 and ICD-11 (AAIDD, 2025b). Dumbo's characteristics, as portrayed in the film, could possibly be consistent with some traits of IDD. Firstly, he is shown to experience difficulty with certain problem-solving tasks, slower learning in some areas compared to his peers, and significant reliance on guidance from others, most notably his mouse friend, for social navigation and daily functioning. His communication is nonverbal, and he initially struggles to adapt to new environments and challenges without support, which aligns with the adaptive behavior limitations associated with IDD (AAIDD, 2025a).

The diagnosis of IDD typically involves the use of standardized assessment tools that measure both intellectual functioning and adaptive behavior (AAIDD, 2025b). Commonly used cognitive assessments include the Wechsler Intelligence Scale for Children (WISC) and the Stanford-Binet Intelligence Scales, which provide an estimate of intellectual ability through tasks assessing reasoning, problem-solving, and memory (Saad & ElAdl, 2019). Adaptive functioning is often evaluated using instruments such as the Vineland Adaptive Behavior Scales (Vineland-3) or the Adaptive Behavior Assessment System (ABAS-3), which examine conceptual, social, and practical life skills (AAIDD, 2025b; Hazarika et al., 2017). Hypothetically applying this to Dumbo, evaluators might use nonverbal adaptations of intelligence tests—given his lack of spoken language—to assess problem-solving and learning ability. Likewise, an adaptive behavior scale completed by his caregiver could capture his social interactions, daily functioning, and ability to adapt to challenges (AAIDD, 2025a; Hazarika et al., 2017). Such assessments would provide a clearer, evidence-based picture of whether Dumbo meets the diagnostic criteria for IDD. Another assessment tool that could be beneficial in Dumbo's case is the Expressive One-Word Picture Vocabulary Test-4 (EOWPVT-4) (Pearson Assessments, n.d.). Given that Dumbo does not present any expressive language ability, this tool could be useful in understanding the scope of his impairment. The EOWPVT-4 was designed to test expressive vocabulary skills from ages two years and older (Pearson Assessments, n.d.). The test takes approximately 15–25 minutes to complete, and the results collected are compared to a normative sample. Specifically, the test presents individuals with color illustrations of objects, actions, or concepts, and they are asked to name them, using one word (Pearson Assessments, n.d.). The test aims to measure acquired vocabulary appropriate to the individual's age. It is also able to screen for early language delays, aphasias, and general cognitive abilities.

Etiology

The following paragraphs will go in depth regarding the etiology of IDD and how this relates to Dumbo's case. Genetic and chromosomal abnormalities are among the most common identifiable causes of IDD (Harris,

2014). These include inherited syndromes such as Down syndrome, Fragile X syndrome, and Williams syndrome, as well as single-gene metabolic disorders like phenylketonuria (PKU) (AAIDD, 2025a; Saad & ElAdl, 2019). In some cases, IDD arises from de novo mutations or chromosomal anomalies, such as trisomy 18, that are not inherited from the parents (National Institute of Child Health and Human Development [NICHHD], 2021).

IDD may also result from harmful exposures or complications during pregnancy and birth. Prenatal factors include maternal infections such as rubella or cytomegalovirus, maternal metabolic disorders, and prenatal exposure to alcohol, which can lead to fetal alcohol spectrum disorders (Centers for Disease Control and Prevention [CDC], 2024; NICHHD, 2021). Perinatal complications—such as oxygen deprivation (hypoxia) during delivery, preterm birth, or low birth weight—can cause brain injury that interferes with cognitive and adaptive development (AAIDD, 2025b; Salvador-Carulla et al., 2011).

Although less common, events occurring after birth can also lead to IDD. These postnatal causes include severe infections such as bacterial meningitis, traumatic brain injury, near-drowning incidents, strokes, or abusive head trauma (CDC, 2024; Hazarika et al., 2017). While postnatal factors account for a smaller percentage of IDD cases, they are often preventable through adequate healthcare, safety measures, and early intervention (Salvador-Carulla et al., 2011). Preventing these injuries is a critical component of reducing the incidence of IDD in childhood.

Exposure to environmental toxins during critical developmental periods can also contribute to IDD. Lead poisoning, mercury exposure, and other neurotoxic agents are known to damage the developing brain and impair cognitive function (CDC, 2024; NICHHD, 2021). Additionally, chronic malnutrition and a lack of sensory or cognitive stimulation in early childhood can hinder brain development, especially in socioeconomically disadvantaged settings (Salvador-Carulla et al., 2011).

The etiology of Dumbo's possible IDD could be speculated based on events depicted in the 1941 film. Given that Dumbo was born with atypical physical features—most notably his unusually large ears—one could infer the possibility of a genetic or congenital syndrome that might also affect cognitive and adaptive functioning (AAIDD, 2025a; Saad & ElAdl, 2019). Although the film does not explicitly depict complications during birth, it is conceivable that prenatal or perinatal factors, such as maternal stress or nutritional deficits within the circus environment, could have influenced his early development (NICHHD, 2021; CDC, 2024). Environmental influences, such as the emotionally stressful and socially isolating conditions he experiences after separation from his mother, may have further hindered his adaptive skill development (Hazarika et al., 2017). While these suggestions remain speculative, they align with recognized categories of IDD etiology, including genetic, prenatal, and environmental contributors.

Treatment/Interventions

Children with IDD are fully capable of experiencing and expressing a wide range of positive emotions, including joy, curiosity, pride, and affection (AAIDD, 2025a; Hazarika et al., 2017). With Dumbo, it is notably apparent that his loving and kind nature is what really causes audiences to empathize with him. Such emotional expressions play a critical role in Dumbo's social and cognitive development, helping him engage with his environment and form meaningful relationships. Developing a secure attachment with a primary caregiver is particularly important for children with IDD, as it provides a foundation of safety and trust that supports exploration, learning, and emotional regulation (CDC, 2024; Saad & ElAdl, 2019). In the case of Dumbo, he has a secure attachment with his mother, which will facilitate his future development and is imperative when it comes to the development and potential success of an individualized intervention plan.

Interventions for children with IDD are most effective when they are individualized, strengths-based, and aimed at enhancing both cognitive and adaptive functioning (AAIDD, 2025a; Bertelli et al., 2015; Hazarika et al., 2017; Saad & ElAdl, 2019). These interventions often include behavioral therapies, speech and language support, occupational therapy, and social skills training, all designed to promote learning, independence, and emotional well-being (Bertelli et al., 2015; CDC, 2024; NICHHD, 2021). In a hypothetical case such as Dumbo, targeted interventions could focus on fostering his problem-solving abilities, social interactions, and emotional regulation, particularly given his early experiences of social isolation and stress. Furthermore, a proposed intervention would be language and speech therapy, which could focus on his verbal development. Moreover, placing Dumbo in an environment where he can socialize with other elephants his age would also be beneficial for him, as he currently only has one mouse friend.

Furthermore, a child-centered play therapy (CCPT) approach would also be suitable (Landreth, 2012). This intervention allows the child to freely explore their needs and wants in a safe playroom environment, with a professional play therapist who facilitates interaction. Perhaps the use of creative-expression materials would allow Dumbo to gain some self-esteem and confidence with regards to his abilities and therefore help him develop in his social domain (Landreth, 2012). It could also prove to be a means to release any inner anxiety or stress he may be feeling from the social isolation and bullying that he has faced. Following Rogers (1951) and Axline's (1991) theory indicates that the child has the ability to self-actualize; it is suggested that the CCPT follows a non-directive approach. Applied to Dumbo, a nurturing and accepting environment—like the support he ultimately receives from the mouse—could help him develop his unique abilities, such as his extraordinary capacity for flight, reflecting his journey toward self-actualization despite early developmental challenges.

Finally, a systemic-family approach is appropriate given that Dumbo is still very young and would benefit from his mother's involvement in the intervention (Harris, 2014). Specifically, Ms. Jumbo would benefit from parental training, which could help her understand what her son is going through and how to deal with it. Together, these approaches underscore the importance of individualized support, emotional attunement, and the promotion of strengths in children with IDD, demonstrating that with appropriate interventions, even significant developmental challenges can be met with resilience and achievement.

Conclusion

From all that has been presented thus far, it can be speculated that Dumbo is a unique and endearing elephant with potential for a bright future ahead of him. He has courageously overcome the anxiety and shame that he feels about his appearance and turned it into a gift. He will also be able to increase his sense of self-worth and self-esteem through CCPT sessions. Regarding his struggles with language and communication, working with a speech therapist would be beneficial for him. Finally, the consistent support from his mother posits as a protective factor for him. Their bond is evidently unbreakable and will help them both cope with his diagnosis of IDD as he grows into adolescence.

References

American Association on Intellectual and Developmental Disabilities. (2025a). *Defining criteria for intellectual disability.* American Association on Intellectual and Developmental Disabilities. https://www.aaidd.org/intellectual--disability/definition

American Association on Intellectual and Developmental Disabilities. (2025b). *FAQs on intellectual disability.* American Association on Intellectual and Developmental Disabilities (AAIDD). https://www.aaidd.org/intellectual--disability/faqs-on-intellectual-disability

Axline, V. (1991). *Play therapy.* Ballantine Books.

Bertelli, M. O., Bianco, A., Piva Merli, M., & Salvador-Carulla, L. (2015). The person-centered health model in intellectual developmental disorders/intellectual disability. *The European Journal of Psychiatry, 29*(4), 239–248. https://doi.org/10.4321/s0213-61632015000400002

Boyd, D. R., & Bee, H. L. (2019). *Lifespan development.* Pearson.

Centers for Disease Control and Prevention. (2024, May 16). *Developmental disability basics.* Child Development. https://www.cdc.gov/child-development/about/developmental-disability-basics.html

Dumbo. (1941). *[film] Directed by B. Sharpsteen.* Walt Disney Studios.

Harris, J. C. (2014). Intellectual disability (intellectual developmental disorder). In *Gabbard's treatments of psychiatric disorders.* American Psychiatric Publishing.

Hazarika, M., Das, S., & Choudhury, S. (2017). Parents' attitude towards children and adolescents with intellectual developmental disorder. *International Journal of Child Development and Mental Health, 5*(1), 11–21.

Landreth, G. L. (2012). *Play therapy: The art of the relationship.* Routledge.

Meyer, A. (2015). Elephants forever. https://wallpapers.com/elephant#:~:text=Thelife%20cycle%20of%20the,%20adolescent%20and%20the%20adult%20elephant.&text=The%20baby%20stage%20lasts%20from,%20and%2010%20years%20of%20age

National Institute of Child Health and Human Development. (2021, November 9). *About intellectual and developmental disabilities (IDDs).* National Institute of Child Health and Human Development. https://www.nichd.nih.gov/health/topics/idds/conditioninfo

Parritz, R. H., & Troy, M. F. (2011). *Disorders of childhood: Development and psychopathology.* Wadsworth Cengage Learning.

Pearson Assessments. (n.d.). Receptive and expressive one-word picture vocabulary tests: Fourth edition. https://www.pearsonclinical.ca/store/caassessments/en/p/receptive-and-expressive-one-word-picture-vocabulary-tests-fourth-edition/P100055000?tab=product-details

Rogers, C. (1951). *Client-centered therapy: Its current practice, implications, and theory.* Houghton Mifflin.

Saad, M. A. E., & ElAdl, A. M. (2019). Defining and determining intellectual disability (intellectual developmental disorder): Insights from DSM-5. *International Journal of Psycho-Educational Sciences, 8*(1), 51–54. https://files.eric.ed.gov/fulltext/ED594326.pdf

Salvador-Carulla, L., Reed, G. M., Vaez-Azizi, L. M., Cooper, S. A., Leal, R. M., Bertelli, M., Adnams, C., Cooray, S., Deb, S., Dirani, L. A., Girimaji, S. C., Katz, G., Kwok, H., Luckasson, R., Simeonsson, R., Walsh, C., Munir, K., & Saxena, S. (2011). Intellectual developmental disorders: Towards a new name, definition and framework for "mental retardation/intellectual disability" in ICD-11. *World Psychiatry, 10*(3), 175–180. https://doi.org/10.1002/j.2051-5545.2011.tb00045.x

Shoshani, J. (2020, October 2). Elephant. *Encyclopedia Britannica*. https://www.britannica.com/animal/elephant-mammal

CHAPTER 3

Little Red Riding Hood

Anna Rombotis and Stella Kossidi

Abstract This chapter explores the character Little Red Riding Hood, from the story Little Red Riding Hood, originally written by Perrault (1697) and then adapted by Grimm and Grimm (*Grimms' household fairy tales: The original 1812 collection*. Suzeteo Enterprises, 2018). Little Red Riding Hood is an only child, a little girl in middle childhood around eight years of age. She is asked by her mother to bring a basket of goods to her grandmother. Her mother instructs her not to talk to strangers on the way to her grandmother's cabin deep in the forest. Little Red is taken advantage of and is in danger from a wolf disguised as her grandmother. Her unique development will be assessed and diagnosed while taking into consideration her emotional, social, physical, and cognitive development. In this vignette, Little Red Riding Hood is diagnosed with post-traumatic stress symptoms (PTS) or post-traumatic stress disorder (PTSD) from her traumatic interactions with the wolf, and is assessed through evaluating her demographics, risk factors, protective factors, attachment style, etiology of the syndrome/disorder, and clinical treatment interventions.

A. Rombotis (✉) • S. Kossidi
Hellenic American University Alumna, Athens, Greece
e-mail: arombotis@hauniv.edu; skossidi@hauniv.edu

A. Sax (ed.), *Understanding Child Psychopathology Through Fairytales*, https://doi.org/10.1007/978-3-032-14097-5_3

Keywords Middle childhood • Risk factors • Protective factors • Attachment style • Post-traumatic stress • Post-traumatic stress disorder

The Story of Little Red Riding Hood

Little Red Riding Hood tells the story of an eight-year-old girl living with her mother in a small village (Ashliman, 2015). One day, her mother asks her to deliver food and wine to her elderly, sick grandmother, who lives deep in the forest. Before sending her off, she warns Red not to veer from the path, fearing that she might trip and spill the contents of her basket (Fig. 3.1).

On her journey, Red encounters the antagonist—the wolf—who exploits her innocence by convincing her to stray from the path to gather flowers for her grandmother. While she is distracted, the wolf rushes ahead, devours the grandmother, and disguises himself in her clothes. When Red arrives, she is deceived by his disguise and is ultimately eaten as well. Fortunately, a huntsman comes to their rescue, cutting open the wolf's stomach to free them both unharmed. The grandmother then recovers, after eating the food and drinking the wine Red brought her.

Varying Versions of the Tale

The story, originally written by Perrault (1697, as cited in Lang, 2017) and later retold by the Brothers Grimm and Grimm (2018, as cited in Ashliman, 2015), remains largely the same but features notable differences. For instance, the Grimms' version introduces the mother's stern warning: "Do not talk to strangers!" (Ashliman, 2015), a moralistic addition not found in Perrault's version.

In the seventeenth century, childhood was understood very differently than it is today. Before formal education systems existed, children's literature was scarce (Marani, 2020), and high child mortality rates in the Middle Ages forced children to mature early (Hühne-Osterloh & Grupe, 1989). Perrault's original tale reflects this reality, delivering a dark message aimed primarily at adults. In his version, Red is manipulated by the wolf in an unsettlingly eroticized narrative, with the author emphasizing her beauty and innocence—a theme far from appropriate for children.

The Grimms' retelling a century later transforms the story into a moral fable for children, emphasizing obedience and caution around strangers.

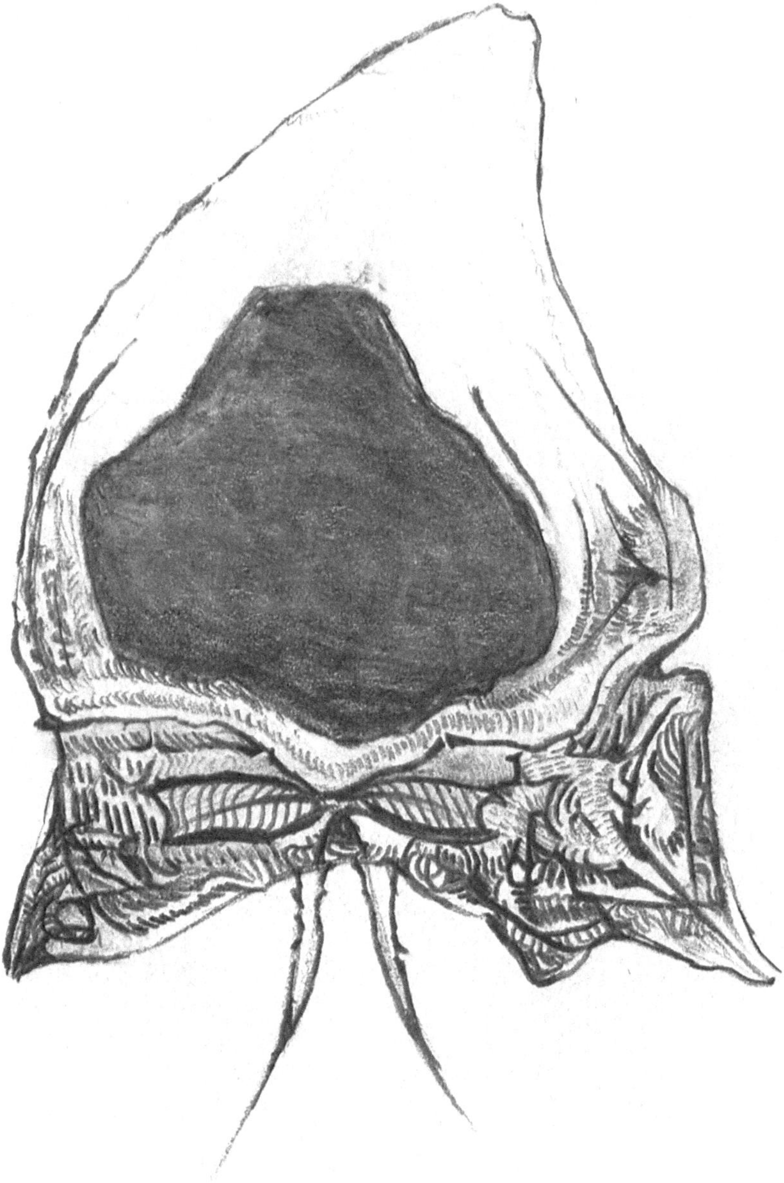

Fig. 3.1 Little Red Riding Hood

The tone shifts from grim satire to lighthearted amusement, replacing tragedy with a hopeful ending.

Demographic Background

From the text, we know that Red is an only child, approximately eight years old, living with her mother in a rural village. Her grandmother resides alone in the forest, while Red's father is never mentioned. Some interpretations speculate that the father figure is embodied by the huntsman in Grimm and Grimm's (2018) version, as he fulfills the role of protector and savior (Ashliman, 2015).

Another theory by Bettelheim (1976) suggests a symbolic split: the father figure exists as both the nurturing, civil huntsman and the dangerous, predatory wolf. Both interpretations align with a child's complex perception of a father figure—protective yet potentially threatening—suggesting that the father's presence lingers in the narrative, albeit concealed.

Psychodynamic Analysis

Red's current development falls under the category of middle childhood. At eight years old, she is beginning to show more sophisticated and complex emotions and social interactions (Boyd & Bee, 2019). Children at this stage often learn to mask their true thoughts or feelings to spare others, and they begin forming a clearer sense of identity shaped by their interests, talents, friendships, and family relationships. They also start to desire privacy and may alternate between confidence and self-doubt (Boyd & Bee, 2019).

In Red's case, her interests, talents, and bonds with her mother and grandmother reflect normal development. However, her self-doubt is evident when she interacts with the wolf disguised as her grandmother, ultimately leading to her being deceived and eaten. Furthermore, according to Boyd and Bee (2019), children of this age typically develop the ability to self-regulate according to parental expectations without constant monitoring. Red has not yet achieved this milestone, as she was unable to fully follow her mother's instructions on her journey.

Socially, middle childhood marks a phase where children begin to join peer groups and gain greater autonomy from parents (Boyd & Bee, 2019). Given that Red lives in a small forest village with limited exposure to peers—and possibly does not attend school due to the story's historical setting—her opportunities for social interaction and forming meaningful friendships may be restricted. Normally, a child of her age would be in grade two or three, gravitating toward peers of the same gender.

Regarding moral development, Red appears to be in Kohlberg's pre-conventional stage, where judgments of right and wrong are based on potential punishment or obedience to rules (as cited in Boyd & Bee, 2019). The story suggests a clear message: when a child disobeys parental expectations, they face negative consequences.

Cognitively, eight-year-olds make significant progress in understanding concepts such as money, responsibility, and cause-and-effect reasoning. Red demonstrates some understanding of responsibility by attempting to deliver the basket to her grandmother. However, her emotions still strongly influence her thinking, as children this age may struggle to make sound judgments when worried, fearful, or angry. This is partly due to the ongoing development of the prefrontal cortex, which is responsible for executive functions like planning, organizing, and decision-making (Boyd & Bee, 2019). The story shows Red struggling with these abilities—she fails to judge the wolf's intentions and mistakes him for her grandmother.

According to Erikson's psychosocial stages (as cited in Boyd & Bee, 2019), Red is in the "industry versus inferiority" stage, where competence is developed through mastering cognitive and motor skills. At this age, children refine fine and gross motor abilities and improve coordination (Boyd & Bee, 2019). Red demonstrates some physical development by walking through the forest while carrying the basket. However, this responsibility may have been too demanding for her level of stamina and motor skills. Traveling long distances through uneven terrain could cause fatigue and distraction, which ultimately contributed to her straying from the path.

Risk Factors

In many fairy tales, risk factors are often presented symbolically. Freud and Jung viewed symbols as figurative representations of unconscious elements, revealing mental messages that cannot be expressed verbally (Settineri et al., 2017). In Little Red Riding Hood, the forest functions as a primary risk factor. Historically, forests have been linked to both human survival and danger, especially in medieval and pre-medieval times when most people lived near wooded areas (Birrell, 1969). Psychologically, the forest can symbolize the unconscious—fertile yet wild, unpredictable, and potentially threatening. It is no coincidence that many fairy-tale protagonists, including Red, Snow White, Hansel and Gretel, and Goldilocks, become "lost" in the woods before returning changed, more cautious, and more domesticated.

The wolf represents another significant risk factor. Hanah and Kaylah (2017) interpret the wolf as a manifestation of Red's internal vulnerability—an externalized threat that exists because of her inability to protect herself, potentially stemming from insufficient protection during her upbringing. Red's life appears to revolve around strong attachments to the females in her family, particularly her mother and grandmother, while her father's absence remains unexplained. A more involved paternal figure might have influenced her ability to recognize danger or respond assertively to it.

Additionally, Red's naiveté and isolation heighten her risk. Living in a small, secluded forest village with little opportunity for peer interaction may have left her socially inexperienced, less equipped to navigate unfamiliar encounters, and more susceptible to manipulation by strangers. The combination of limited social exposure, a missing father figure, and a trusting nature creates an environment where Red is particularly vulnerable to danger, both real and symbolic.

Protective Factors

Red's relationships with her mother, grandmother, and the huntsman stand out as important protective factors in the fairy tale. She clearly shows responsiveness toward her mother, readily agreeing to take the care basket on her journey to her grandmother's house. Additionally, her positive bond with her grandmother is highlighted by the gift of the red hood. While there is limited information about Red's connection with the huntsman, it can be inferred that they share some familiarity, given that he ultimately saves her life. Beyond these relationships, Red's kind and good-natured spirit also serves as a protective factor, equipping her to build meaningful relationships in the future.

Attachment Style

Regarding attachment, Red appears to have a secure attachment style with her mother. The story shows her mother trusting Red with the responsibility of delivering the care basket and asking her to promise that she will stay on the path—demonstrating the mother's caring and protective nature. Secure attachment is also characterized by a child's ability to separate from their caregiver, which is evident as Red confidently sets out on her journey alone.

The role of a father is also significant in early childhood attachment, often involving opportunities for bonding through physical activities (Boyd & Bee, 2019). However, Red's father is absent from the story, which may contribute to her naivety and readiness to trust the wolf.

Diagnosis

Sigmund Freud's psychoanalytic theory posits that all human behavior is motivated by sexuality (as cited in Boyd & Bee, 2019). Central to this theory are the concepts of the id, ego, and superego. In the story, the wolf represents the id—driven purely by instinctual desires such as hunger, as illustrated when he "threw himself upon Little Red Riding Hood" (Ashliman, 2015). Red's mother embodies the superego, cautioning her daughter to stay on the path, thereby instilling moral awareness and protecting her from impulsive urges. Red herself symbolizes the ego, struggling to mediate between the wolf's temptations (id) and her mother's warnings (superego) (Bonfiglio, 2017).

Hanah and Kaylah (2017) offer a compelling psychological interpretation of Little Red Riding Hood, suggesting that the wolf symbolizes an internal threat within Red's psyche—rooted in her inability to protect herself emotionally due to insufficient care during her upbringing. This view shifts the tale's moral from a simple warning against straying from the path or talking to strangers, toward an understanding of Red's vulnerability and emotional risk. Their theory proposes that Red could be at risk of developing post-traumatic stress symptoms or disorder (PTS or PTSD) following the traumatic encounter with the wolf at her grandmother's house.

Because Red is a young child, her PTS symptoms would likely manifest as internalizing behaviors rather than overt externalizing ones, which can complicate diagnosis. Therefore, a thorough assessment should combine multiple tools such as interviews, self-reports, rating scales, physiological measures, clinical observations, and evidence-based instruments (Parritz & Troy, 2011). In Red's case, a holistic approach would be most effective, incorporating observations, interviews with both Red and her mother, and the use of validated measures such as the Trauma Symptom Checklist for Young Children (TSCYC) (Briere et al., 2001). The TSCYC includes

90 items designed to assess trauma symptoms across various exposure types in children aged 3–12, based on caregiver reports. Briere et al. (2001) report strong reliability and psychometric properties for the scale.

A significant challenge in diagnosing trauma-related disorders in children is the frequent lack of concurrence between parent and child reports. This may stem from the child's difficulty articulating anxiety, reluctance to disclose distress, parental unawareness of symptoms, or parental distress themselves (Parritz & Troy, 2011).

Etiology

PTS and PTSD fall within the spectrum of anxiety disorders (Parritz & Troy, 2011). Vulnerability to developing anxiety-based disorders arises from a complex interplay of factors, including genetics, neurophysiological changes, temperament, attachment style, cognitive processes, negative affect, environmental influences, life events, and family context.

From the story, it is clear that Red is a charming girl with a natural ability to befriend others, as the narrative states, "everyone who saw her liked her" (Grimm & Grimm, 2018, as cited in Ashliman, 2015). Growing up with this reputation can create pressure to maintain a likable and "harming" persona. Hanah and Kaylah (2017) propose that this fixed mindset acts as a defense mechanism, protecting Red from anxiety. However, this very defense may have impaired her ability to recognize the wolf's true, harmful intentions, ultimately leading to her traumatic encounter when the wolf devoured her at her grandmother's house.

Such trauma can profoundly affect Red's development and may trigger PTS symptoms. These symptoms can influence arousal, behavior, emotional regulation, perception, cognition, and interpersonal adjustment (Parritz & Troy, 2011). Common manifestations include recurrent memories or flashbacks of the trauma, hallucinations or illusions related to the event, intense fear or horror, sleep disturbances, hyperarousal, and increased clinginess to caregivers. For Red, these symptoms might emerge during her journey to her grandmother's house, while at the house, or upon exposure to reminders of the trauma.

To meet diagnostic criteria for PTSD, symptoms must persist over a sustained period. Given that Red's traumatic experience resulted partly from her naivety and impaired judgment, she may experience feelings of guilt, shame, helplessness, and terror. She might even withdraw from social interactions, fearing a recurrence of trauma. Without intervention, her symptoms could worsen, potentially impairing her relationships, learning abilities, and self-regulation (Parritz & Troy, 2011). The road to recovery from PTSD is closely paved by resilience—the capacity to adapt and bounce back after adversity. Red's own resilience will be a crucial factor in her healing journey.

Treatment/Interventions

For anxiety-based disorders, it is best to employ preventative measures before reaching treatment options. However, this is often challenging, given the internalizing nature of these conditions. Consequently, treatment typically involves a combined approach incorporating psychodynamic therapy, play therapy, and cognitive-behavioral therapy (CBT). Among these, CBT has gained prominence because it addresses multiple facets: psychoeducation for both the child and parent about the disorder; somatic management aimed at reducing physiological symptoms related to anxiety; cognitive restructuring to challenge and modify maladaptive thoughts; problem-solving to develop coping strategies; gradual, controlled exposure to feared situations; and relapse prevention by strengthening anxiety management skills (Parritz & Troy, 2011).

In Red's case, involving her mother—and potentially her grandmother, given their close relationship and shared trauma—would be crucial for a comprehensive CBT approach. When treating PTSD, it is essential to provide immediate crisis intervention alongside ongoing support tailored to the child's needs.

Key treatment goals for Red would include re-establishing a sense of safety, particularly when navigating the woods and visiting her grandmother's house—the sites of her trauma. Another priority would be to reduce the intensity of her emotional and physiological reactions triggered by reminders or memories of the traumatic event. Lastly, therapy should help Red process and make meaning of her experience while simultaneously supporting her caregivers throughout the healing journey (Scheeringa & Gaensbauer, 2000).

Conclusion

The story of Little Red Riding Hood is a timeless tale, still read to children today. Psychologically, it portrays a young girl cherished for her charming nature, who struggles to live up to this ideal and ultimately faces a traumatic encounter with the wolf. This event places her at risk of developing PTS or PTSD. Fortunately, Red's secure attachment to her mother provides a strong foundation for healing and support throughout the treatment process. CBT focused on managing her anxiety and reducing intense emotional and physiological reactions to trauma would be beneficial. The involvement of her grandmother, who shares a close bond with Red and experienced the trauma alongside her, would also enhance her recovery.

Red's mother will need to support her in reaching important developmental milestones, especially in peer socialization. Additionally, therapy might explore the impact of her absent father on her emotional well-being. Ultimately, immediate crisis management is crucial to help Red make sense of her experiences and foster healthy coping, increasing the likelihood of a positive recovery.

References

Ashliman, D. L. (2015). Little red cap. https://sites.pitt.edu/~dash/grimm026.html

Bettelheim, B. (1976). *The uses of enchantment: The meaning and importance of fairy tales*. Knopf.

Birrell, J. (1969). Peasant craftsmen in the medieval forest. *The Agricultural History Review, 17*(2), 91–107. http://www.jstor.org/stable/40273323

Bonfiglio, T. P. (2017). *The psychopathology of American capitalism*. Palgrave Macmillan.

Boyd, D. R., & Bee, H. L. (2019). *Lifespan development*. Pearson.

Briere, J., Johnson, K., Bissada, A., Damon, L., Crouch, J., Gil, E., Hanson, R., & Ernst, V. (2001). The trauma symptom checklist for young children (TSCYC): Reliability and association with abuse exposure in a multi-site study. *Child Abuse & Neglect, 25*(8), 1001–1014. https://doi.org/10.1016/s0145-2134(01)00253-8

Grimm, J., & Grimm, W. (2018). *Grimms' household fairy tales: The original 1812 collection*. Suzeteo Enterprises.

Hanah, D., & Kaylah, J. (2017). Severance of the parent-child structure and little red riding hood. *International Journal of Guidance and Counselling, 3*(1), 57–67. https://www.globalscienceresearchjournals.org/articles/severance-of-the-parentchild-structure-and-little-red-riding-hood.pdf

Hühne-Osterloh, G., & Grupe, G. (1989). Causes of infant mortality in the Middle Ages revealed by chemical and palaeopathological analyses of skeletal remains. *Zeitschrift für Morphologie und Anthropologie, 77*(3), 247–258. https://doi.org/10.1127/zma/77/1989/247

Lang, A. (2017). *The blue fairy book*. Open Road Integrated Media.
Marani, N. (2020). Week 4: Children's literature history. https://docenti.unimc.it/noemi.marani/teaching/2020/22793/files/week-4
Parritz, R. H., & Troy, M. F. (2011). *Disorders of childhood: Development and psychopathology*. Wadsworth Cengage Learning.
Scheeringa, M. S., & Gaensbauer, T. J. (2000). Posttraumatic stress disorder. In C. H. Zeanah Jr. (Ed.), *Handbook of infant mental health* (pp. 369–381). The Guilford Press. https://psycnet.apa.org/record/2000-07057-023
Settineri, S., Merlo, E. M., Turiaco, F., & Mento, C. (2017). The symbol theory in S. Freud, C.G. Jung and C. S. Peirce. *Mediterranean Journal of Clinical Psychology, 5*(2), 1–21. https://www.researchgate.net/publication/319260864_The_symbol_theory_in_S_Freud_C_G_Jung_and_C_S_Peirce

CHAPTER 4

Pinocchio

Aysan Jahankhah and Anna Rombotis

Abstract This chapter explores the character Pinocchio from the story Pinocchio, written by Collodi (*The adventures of Pinocchio.* London, New York, 1989). Pinocchio is a wooden puppet made by Geppetto, a wood craftsman. Pinocchio, who is given life by the Blue Fairy, must prove to her and his father (Geppetto) his moral reasoning, resilience, and ability to be a genuine real boy. Pinocchio is in middle childhood and is seven years old. Pinocchio learns to experience the real world through adventures and misadventures, often getting into trouble and being prone to lying, with undesirable company. When Pinocchio lies, his nose grows longer and longer, the bigger the lie becomes. His unique development will be assessed and diagnosed while taking into consideration his emotional, social, physical, and cognitive development. In this vignette, Pinocchio is diagnosed with oppositional defiant disorder (ODD) and is assessed through evaluating his demographics, risk factors, protective factors, attachment style, etiology of the syndrome/disorder, and clinical treatment interventions.

A. Jahankhah (✉) • A. Rombotis
Hellenic American University Alumna, Athens, Greece
e-mail: ajahankhah@hauniv.edu; arombotis@hauniv.edu

A. Sax (ed.), *Understanding Child Psychopathology Through Fairytales*, https://doi.org/10.1007/978-3-032-14097-5_4

Keywords Middle childhood • Moral reasoning • Resilience • Risk factors • Protective factors • Attachment style • Oppositional defiant disorder

The Story of Pinocchio

Pinocchio, the children's book written by Carlo Collodi and first published in 1883, tells the enchanting tale of a small wooden puppet crafted by the humble woodcarver Geppetto. Miraculously brought to life by the Blue Fairy, Pinocchio embarks on a journey filled with adventures and misadventures as he strives to become a real boy (Fig. 4.1). To fulfill this dream, he must prove himself courageous, selfless, and sincere—qualities set as conditions by the Blue Fairy. However, newly exposed to the world, Pinocchio is vulnerable to manipulation and often finds himself led astray, getting into trouble along the way. Known for his tendency to lie, Pinocchio's nose grows longer each time he tells a falsehood. Guiding him through his journey is Mr. Jiminy Cricket, an anthropomorphic cricket who acts as Pinocchio's conscience and mentor. Ultimately, Pinocchio's selfless sacrifice to save Geppetto demonstrates his growth in bravery and sincerity, enabling him to achieve his heartfelt wish and become a real boy (Collodi, 1989).

Demographic Background

Pinocchio originates from a small Italian village in Tuscany. While his exact age is not specified, his recent enrollment in school suggests he is approximately seven years old. As a wooden puppet brought to life, Pinocchio is effectively an adopted child, with Geppetto acting as his single father. Geppetto's limited formal education and modest occupation imply a lower socioeconomic status (SES), reflected in their simple home environment lacking libraries or books.

Psychodynamic Analysis

The following paragraphs will delve into the psychodynamic analysis of Pinocchio's characters based on the social, emotional, cognitive, and physical domains. Socially, Pinocchio benefits from a loving father and supportive companions, yet he remains highly impressionable and easily swayed by negative influences. Based on Erikson's psychosocial theory of

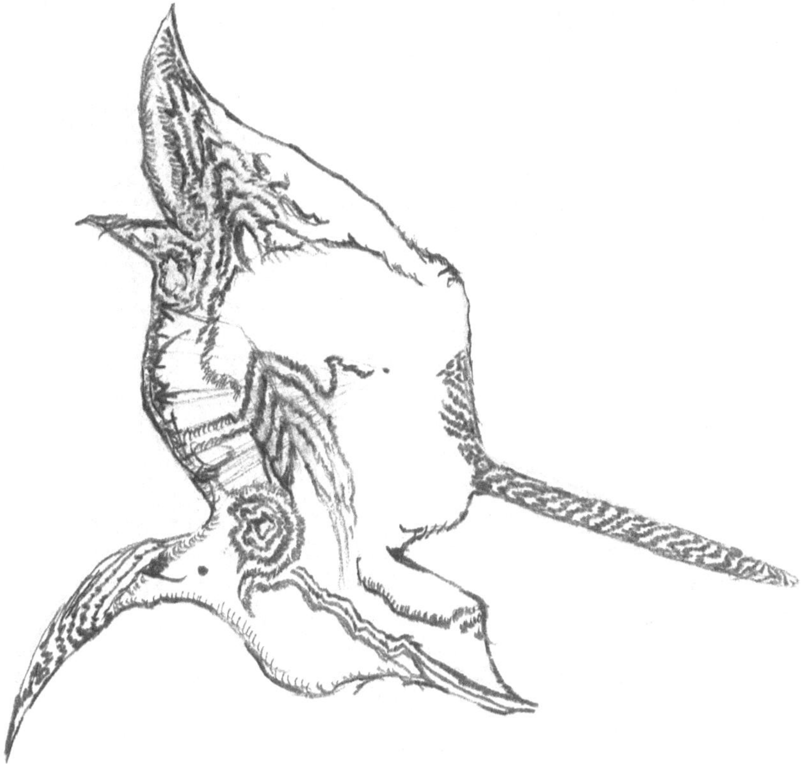

Fig. 4.1 Pinocchio

development (1963), one's personality changes in response to social crises at various developmental stages (as cited by Boyd & Bee, 2019). The young Pinocchio can be categorized in the Industry versus Inferiority stage, whereby his peers are important in this stage. Peer relationships at this age are critical for developing competence and self-esteem. While his friendship with Lampwick initially fosters a sense of confidence, it also exposes him to risky situations. His susceptibility to peer pressure highlights an unresolved social vulnerability that leaves him open to manipulation despite a supportive home environment.

Emotionally, Pinocchio's moral compass is underdeveloped, consistent with Kohlberg's Preconventional stage of moral reasoning. Based on

Kohlberg's theory of moral development, there are three phases of moral development, with each stage having two substages (1984, as cited by Boyd & Bee, 2019). In Pinocchio's case, his decisions are guided by immediate consequences rather than internalized values, making it difficult for him to distinguish right from wrong until faced with repercussions, such as the threat of turning into a donkey. His limited emotional regulation contributes to impulsivity, which in turn perpetuates poor decision-making and moral naivety.

Additionally, to better understand children's moral reasoning, it is equally crucial to comprehend their cognitive functioning. Based on Piaget and Inhelder (1969) theory of cognitive development, infants form their own knowledge through experiences, and their cognitive abilities advance through various phases. The egocentric Pinocchio was moving from the Preoperational stage, when he was pushed outside of his own viewpoints, to the Concrete Operational stage, where he began to become less egocentric and more aware of the outside world and others' opinions (Boyd & Bee, 2019). This is supported by the fact that Pinocchio initially followed his selfish desires to visit Pleasure Island, but as he grew to understand the world and its mishaps, he returned to his father and, in a selfless act, gave his life to save him from the whale's belly at the bottom of the ocean. His developing cognitive skills ultimately allow for more measured problem-solving, though they emerge only after experiencing the consequences of his earlier choices.

Physically, Pinocchio's journey reflects the embodiment of his psychological struggles. His wooden form, vulnerable to transformation and external control, symbolizes the immaturity of his personality structures as described in Freud's model of the id, ego, and superego. The id drives his pursuit of pleasure, while the superego, personified by Mr. Cricket, struggles to assert moral guidance. Over time, his ego strengthens, enabling him to balance personal desires with social expectations, culminating in his transformation into a real boy—a physical manifestation of his integrated emotional, cognitive, and moral development.

Risk Factors

Several factors in Pinocchio's background increase his risk of developing psychopathology, including parenting style, educational level, SES, and trauma. Geppetto's parenting style aligns most closely with a permissive or indulgent approach, where he acted more like a friend than an authoritative parent. He provided limited guidance or direction, imposed few rules, and exercised minimal discipline (Boyd & Bee, 2019). While Geppetto was warm, nurturing, and communicative, his low expectations and leniency may have contributed negatively. Research indicates that children at risk for oppositional defiant disorder (ODD) often have parents perceived as less competent and less assertive in managing behavioral problems (Speltz et al., 1995). Geppetto's apparent lack of confidence and assertiveness in handling Pinocchio's misbehavior could have exacerbated these risks.

Additionally, Geppetto's lifestyle suggests a low educational attainment; his home lacks books and libraries, and his profession does not require formal education. Studies show that low parental education, especially maternal education, correlates with increased symptoms of ODD and attention deficit hyperactivity disorder (ADHD), as well as a higher incidence of negative life events in families facing non-optimal circumstances (Rydell, 2010). SES further compounds these risks—children from low-SES families tend to exhibit more psychopathology than peers from higher-SES backgrounds. For instance, compared to medium-SES groups, low-SES children score higher on internalizing and externalizing symptoms and display poorer social competence (Pérez-Marfil et al., 2020).

Moreover, Pinocchio's experience of being kidnapped constitutes a significant traumatic event during early development. Interestingly, trauma such as kidnapping does not always lead to psychopathology; some research highlights an association with increased resilience. A study involving Iraqi refugee children in the United States found that those who had been kidnapped exhibited higher resilience compared to non-kidnapped peers (Wright et al., 2017).

Protective Factors

Despite the presence of multiple risk factors and a challenging environment, Pinocchio demonstrated notable resilience, managing to remain competent, functional, and positively adaptive to his surroundings. He exhibited effective coping strategies in response to traumatic events (Parritz & Troy, 2011). Several protective factors contributed to this resilience.

Firstly, Pinocchio had a good temperament, which facilitated emotional regulation and adaptability. Additionally, he benefited from a supportive and warm social environment. His father, Geppetto, provided affection and care, and the presence of their pets—Virgo the cat and their fish—offered emotional comfort and a sense of stability. These relationships played a significant role in mitigating the impact of risk factors, fostering Pinocchio's self-esteem and nurturing his developing sense of self-efficacy. Overall, despite the obstacles encountered in his journey toward becoming a real boy, Pinocchio was able to overcome challenges and ultimately demonstrated bravery, honesty, and selflessness.

Attachment Style

Pinocchio's lack of a female parental figure likely had a significant impact on his development and may have contributed to his psychopathology. Attachment refers to the deep and enduring emotional bond formed between a child and their caregiver during the early years of life. This bond profoundly influences various aspects of human functioning, including the mind, body, emotions, relationships, and core values.

Children who do not develop secure attachments with their caregivers often face numerous challenges throughout life and may struggle to establish healthy attachments with their own children in the future. Typically, during the first year of life, an attachment relationship is formed that reflects the degree to which infants feel safety, comfort, and affection from their caregivers. The caregiver's availability, responsiveness, or unpredictability critically shapes the nature of this attachment.

Importantly, the type of attachment formed during these early years can have lasting effects on neurological development, emotional regulation, and social adaptation (Parritz & Troy, 2011). Research shows that individuals diagnosed with conduct disorder (CD) or ODD are significantly more likely to have insecure or disorganized attachment styles compared to those without these disorders (Speltz et al., 1995). These insecure attachments often result from failures to form healthy bonds with primary caregivers in infancy.

Since Pinocchio effectively "started his life" at the age of seven, he likely missed the crucial window for forming secure attachments with a primary caregiver, putting him at risk for an attachment disorder. Disruptions in early caregiver-infant relationships have been linked to neuroendocrine, neurochemical, and behavioral alterations that persist into adulthood. Changes in neurotrophic factor levels during critical developmental stages can result in long-term modifications to neuronal plasticity, increasing vulnerability to psychopathology (Cirulli et al., 2003).

Diagnosis and Assessment

Despite Pinocchio's resilience, he exhibited several symptoms consistent with ODD, a condition characterized primarily by a persistent pattern of defiant, disobedient, and hostile behavior toward authority figures, as well as violation of social norms and the rights of others (American Psychiatric Association, 2013). Pinocchio's behavior—such as (1) frequently blaming others for his mistakes, (2) refusing to comply with adult requests and social rules, and (3) often arguing with adults—suggests significant difficulties in social, academic, and family functioning. These symptoms indicate that Pinocchio likely met criteria for ODD, though further clinical assessment would be necessary to evaluate the frequency, intensity, and pervasiveness of these behaviors for a definitive diagnosis and to guide appropriate intervention.

Additionally, Pinocchio's frequent school absenteeism signals impaired academic functioning, commonly associated with ODD symptomatology, and highlights the impact his behavioral challenges had on his overall development.

Etiology

According to Parritz and Troy (2011), the etiology of ODD is multifactorial, involving parental characteristics, child-specific factors (such as gender, temperament, and attachment style), peer influences, sociocultural environment, trauma exposure, neurological factors, and genetics. The transactional model proposed by Greene et al. (2003) emphasizes the interaction of multiple risk domains contributing to externalizing disorders like ODD. This model suggests that the greater the accumulation of risk factors, the higher the likelihood of developing the disorder.

In Pinocchio's case, parental factors likely played a significant role. Geppetto's permissive parenting style, characterized by limited supervision and low assertiveness, may have exacerbated behavioral issues by failing to provide consistent guidance and discipline. ODD tends to be more prevalent in boys, aligning with Pinocchio's profile (Parritz & Troy, 2011). Furthermore, children exhibiting high sensation-seeking behaviors, increased arousal, and lower harm avoidance—traits evident in Pinocchio's adventurous and impulsive nature—are at an elevated risk for ODD.

Adoption at an older age is also associated with increased vulnerability to developing ODD, which fits Pinocchio's background as a wooden puppet coming "to life" and entering the social world later than typical children. While genetic factors often contribute to ODD risk, this explanation is less applicable for Pinocchio due to his non-human origins.

Treatment/Interventions

Treatment for ODD often centers on family-based approaches, complemented by individual therapy. Family-focused therapy aims to improve parent-child interactions by enhancing cooperation, communication, and mutual understanding among family members (Parritz & Troy, 2011). A particularly effective method is parent-child interaction therapy (PCIT), where parents receive real-time coaching from a therapist while interacting with their child, often through a one-way mirror and an "ear bug" audio device (Bjørseth & Wichstrøm, 2016). This approach enables parents to learn positive reinforcement techniques, strengthens the parent-child bond, and reduces problematic behaviors.

Individual counseling for the child can foster healthier emotional expression and anger management skills, supporting more adaptive behavior (Parritz & Troy, 2011). Additionally, interventions focusing on enhancing social adaptability and peer engagement can further help children with ODD improve their interpersonal relationships and overall functioning.

Conclusion

In summary, Pinocchio's life was marked by significant challenges rooted in his unique origins, family demographics—including low SES and limited parental education—and his behavioral symptoms consistent with ODD. Despite these risk factors, Pinocchio demonstrated remarkable resilience, maintaining competence and adapting positively to his environment. His ability to recover and grow following traumatic experiences reflects a strong capacity for resilience.

Ultimately, Pinocchio's selfless act of sacrificing himself for Geppetto reveals his moral growth, bravery, and leadership, culminating in his transformation into a real boy. His journey highlights the complex interplay between risk factors, protective influences, and personal development in overcoming adversity.

References

American Psychiatric Association. (2013). *Diagnostic and statistical manual of mental disorders* (5th ed.). American Psychiatric Association.

Bjørseth, Å., & Wichstrøm, L. (2016). Effectiveness of parent-child interaction therapy (PCIT) in the treatment of young children's behaviour problems. A randomized controlled study. *PLoS One, 11*(9), e0159845. https://doi.org/10.1371/journal.pone.0159845

Boyd, D. R., & Bee, H. L. (2019). *Lifespan development.* Pearson.

Cirulli, F., Berry, A., & Alleva, E. (2003). Early disruption of the mother–infant relationship: Effects on brain plasticity and implications for psychopathology. *Neuroscience & Biobehavioural Reviews, 27*(2), 73–82. https://doi.org/10.1016/S0149-7634(03)000101

Collodi, C. (1989). *The adventures of Pinocchio.* London.

Erikson, E. H. (1963). *Childhood and society* (2nd ed.). Norton.

Greene, R. W., Ablon, J. S., & Goring, J. C. (2003). A transactional model of oppositional behaviour. *Journal of Psychosomatic Research, 55*(1), 67–75. https://doi.org/10.1016/s0022-3999(02)00585-8

Parritz, R. H., & Troy, M. F. (2011). *Disorders of childhood: Development and psychopathology.* Wadsworth Cengage Learning.

Pérez-Marfil, M. N., Fernández-Alcántara, M., Fasfous, A. F., Burneo-Garcés, C., Pérez-García, M., & Cruz-Quintana, F. (2020). Influence of socio-economic status on psychopathology in Ecuadorian children. *Frontiers in Psychiatry, 11*, 43. https://doi.org/10.3389/fpsyt.2020.00043

Piaget, J., & Inhelder, B. (1969). *The psychology of the child.* Basic Books.

Rydell, A. M. (2010). Family factors and children's disruptive behaviour: An investigation of links between demographic characteristics, negative life events and symptoms of ODD and ADHD. *Social Psychiatry and Psychiatric Epidemiology, 45*(2), 233–244. https://doi.org/10.1007/s00127-009-0060-2

Speltz, M. L., De Klyen, M., & Greenberg, M. T. (1995). Clinic referral for oppositional defiant disorder: Relative significance of attachment and behavioural variables. *Journal of Abnormal Child Psycholology, 23*, 487–507. https://doi.org/10.1007/BF01447210

Wright, A. M., Talia, Y. R., Aldhalimi, A., Broadbridge, C. L., Jamil, H., Lumley, M. A., Pole, N., Arnetz, B. B., & Arnetz, J. E. (2017). Kidnapping and mental health in Iraqi refugees: The role of resilience. *Journal of Immigrant and Minority Health, 19*(1), 98–107. https://doi.org/10.1007/s10903-015-0340-8

CHAPTER 5

Hansel and Gretel

Grace Zografaki and Anna Rombotis

Abstract This chapter explores the characters of Hansel and Gretel, from the story written by Grimm brothers in the seventeenth century. Hansel and Gretel are in middle childhood, about seven and ten years of age, and are abandoned by their father and stepmother. Although initiated by their stepmother, the children are sent into the forest, as their parents cannot afford to feed them. As they find themselves lost in the forest, a bird guides them to a witch's house made of bread, cakes, and sugary treats. With starving gluttony, as they begin to nibble on the house, the witch appears and invites them into the house, only with motives to devour them both with the intention of baking them in her oven. Hansel and Gretel are treated cruelly by the witch, and both display their resilience by escaping from her and returning safely to their home to find their father. Their unique development will be assessed and diagnosed while taking into consideration their emotional, social, physical, and cognitive development. In this vignette, Hansel and Gretel are diagnosed with post-traumatic stress disorder (PTSD) and/or major depressive disorder (MDD) and are assessed through evaluating their demographics, risk

G. Zografaki (✉) • A. Rombotis
Hellenic American University Alumna, Athens, Greece
e-mail: czografaki@hauniv.edu; arombotis@hauniv.edu

A. Sax (ed.), *Understanding Child Psychopathology Through Fairytales*, https://doi.org/10.1007/978-3-032-14097-5_5

factors, protective factors, attachment style, etiology of the syndrome/ disorder, and clinical treatment interventions.

Keywords Middle childhood • Abandonment • Gluttony • Cruelty • Risk factors • Protective factors • Attachment style • Post-traumatic stress disorder • Major depressive disorder

The Story of Hansel and Gretel

Hansel and Gretel is a dark fairy tale collected by the Brothers Grimm, first published in the early nineteenth century (Grimm & Grimm, 2018). It is a haunting story that explores themes of child abandonment, starvation, slavery, and even hints of cannibalism. The narrative opens with a poor woodcutter's family suffering through a devastating famine. The father lives with his second wife and two children from his previous marriage: Hansel, the boy, and Gretel, the girl, both roughly between seven and ten years old (Fig. 5.1).

Faced with starvation, the stepmother urges the father to abandon the children in the forest, arguing they cannot afford to feed four people when food is scarce even for the adults. After some hesitation, the father reluctantly agrees. At their first attempt to leave the children, Hansel overhears the plan and cleverly marks a trail with white stones, allowing the siblings to find their way back home.

The second time, however, the stepmother locks the stones away, forcing Hansel to leave a trail of breadcrumbs instead—only to have the birds devour them. Lost deep in the unfamiliar forest, the children wander for hours until they spot a bird and decide to follow it. The bird leads them to a strange house made entirely of bread, cakes, and sugary treats.

Overcome with hunger and temptation, Hansel and Gretel begin nibbling on the edible walls. Their actions catch the attention of the witch who inhabits the house. She lures them inside with sinister intentions: to fatten Hansel up and eventually eat him. The witch imprisons Hansel in a cage, feeding him rich food to fatten him, while forcing Gretel to serve as her maid, tending to chores like cooking and stoking the fire.

In the story's climax, the witch prepares to bake the children alive in her oven, but Gretel outsmarts her and pushes her into the flames instead. Afterward, Gretel gathers the witch's treasures—pearls and precious stones—and, with the help of a little duck, guides Hansel safely back home. Upon their return, the siblings find their father, who has been

Fig. 5.1 Hansel and Gretel

grieving and worrying about them throughout their absence. The family joyfully reunites, and they learn that the stepmother has died while they were gone (Grimm & Grimm, 2018).

Demographic Background

Several details in the story indicate that Gretel is younger than Hansel, supported by Hansel's protective role—he "took his little sister by the hand" (Grimm & Grimm, 2018). The family structure reveals that the children's biological father is present, while their biological mother died when they were very young, leading to the father's remarriage. Unfortunately, the stepmother does not provide care or affection but instead encourages abandonment.

The father's occupation as a "poor woodcutter" explains the family's precarious financial situation. The widespread famine exacerbates their poverty, leaving the family without sufficient food to support all four members, and ultimately driving the desperate decision to abandon the children.

Psychodynamic Analysis

According to Erikson (1963) children aged seven to ten face the psychosocial crisis of Industry versus Inferiority, which centers on developing competence through productive activities such as schoolwork and peer competition. In Hansel and Gretel, however, it is clear that the children do not attend school. This absence of formal education and peer interaction likely hinders their social and emotional development, depriving them of essential environmental stimuli. The famine and their father's low-income job may have forced them to help with household tasks instead.

Fortunately, Hansel and Gretel had each other, and sibling relationships can foster self-regulation, emotional awareness, and skill development through mutual support (Stormshak et al., 2009).

Scholars often link this tale to the Great Famine of 1315–1317, which ravaged Europe from Russia to Italy (Jordan, 1996). Volcanic eruptions in Southeast Asia and New Zealand triggered climate changes, leading to harvest failures, widespread starvation, and desperate acts such as child abandonment and cannibalism. Historical records note extreme behaviors, including voluntary starvation by the elderly to preserve resources for the young, and exhumation of bodies for food (Jordan, 1996).

These harsh conditions likely impaired children's physical development. Nutritional deficits during this critical period can cause expressive speech delays, poor visual-spatial short-term memory, and increased anxiety (Miranda et al., 2007). Despite these hardships, Hansel and Gretel demonstrate advanced motor skills: they navigate dense woods over long distances and display the stamina and cunning needed to escape the witch's grasp.

Regarding cognitive development, Piaget and Inhelder (1969) describe the concrete operational stage as when children develop organized, logical thinking about concrete events, show greater empathy, and improve selective attention (as cited by Boyd & Bee, 2019). Gretel's reasoning and understanding of the witch's malicious intent, culminating in her shoving the witch into the oven, exemplify these skills. She also exhibits spatial awareness in judging the witch's size to ensure she fits inside the oven. Hansel's clever ruse of offering a bone instead of his finger to fool the witch also highlights his emerging cognitive sophistication.

Risk Factors

Several risk factors in Hansel and Gretel could increase the siblings' vulnerability to psychopathology. Their lack of schooling, likely due to famine and poverty, limits cognitive and social development. Low socioeconomic status is a well-established social risk factor linked to poor developmental outcomes (Boyd & Bee, 2019). Children in impoverished families often live in disorganized, stressful environments, with less intellectual stimulation and harsher parenting styles (Roubinov & Boyce, 2017; Hoffman, 2003).

Parenting style is a crucial risk factor. Poverty combined with neglectful or harsh parenting increases children's risk for mental health issues (Parritz & Troy, 2011). In the tale, the stepmother's cruelty dominates the household, despite the father's affection, as he lacks authority. The children suffer emotional neglect and insecurity, demonstrated by being abandoned twice in the forest—an act showing indifference to their safety and emotional needs. Such abandonment likely provoked fear, anxiety, and trauma, especially considering their young age and vulnerability.

Research indicates that children under eight show intense anxiety and sleep disturbances after abandonment or separation, while those between 9 and 12 can initially fear separation but usually overcome it (Chiracu, 2016). Hansel and Gretel, though young, show resilience that may stem from previous separations or a secure attachment to their deceased biological mother.

The loss of a parent at a young age also increases the risk of depression, especially for girls under 11 (Patten, 1991). The children's mother died early, and their father remarried a stepmother who lacked nurturing qualities. This combination of loss, neglect, and poverty presents significant risk factors that could negatively impact Hansel's and Gretel's psychological development and increase their susceptibility to psychopathology.

Protective Factors

Despite living in a challenging and impoverished environment, Hansel and Gretel benefited from several protective factors that supported their survival and resilience. Most notably, their strong cognitive abilities and mutual support proved crucial in overcoming the dangers they faced. As Stormshak et al. (2009) emphasize, siblings can stimulate one another's development by providing positive emotional support and facilitating skill acquisition. This dynamic is clearly demonstrated in the tale, as Hansel and Gretel consistently collaborated, encouraging each other and devising strategies to navigate their hardships.

Their inherent resilience and positive temperaments also served as important protective traits, enabling them to withstand the trauma and uncertainty of their situation. Moreover, despite their father's poor decision to remarry and his apparent inability to confront his wife's cruelty, he remained a significant and favorable figure in their lives. Their choice to return to him after escaping the witch, and his distraught reaction to their absence, indicate a secure and loving bond. The presence of these protective factors ultimately empowered Hansel and Gretel to survive and find safety by the story's end.

Attachment Style

The attachment patterns portrayed in the story are complex and somewhat unusual. Hansel and Gretel had the opportunity to form a secure attachment with their biological father, who had been a consistent presence since their birth. This is supported by his initial resistance to abandoning them in the forest, reflecting genuine concern and emotional connection.

In contrast, the children's relationship with their stepmother is characterized by emotional neglect and rejection. Her later arrival and harsh treatment likely resulted in an insecure-avoidant attachment style, in which the children avoid seeking comfort or expressing a preference toward her (Boyd & Bee, 2019). This insecure attachment may have contributed to the children's vulnerability but was counterbalanced by their secure connection to their father.

Diagnosis and Assessment

Hansel and Gretel have endured numerous significant barriers throughout their lives, which may contribute to a range of potential psychopathologies. Most notably, the traumatic experiences of living through famine, being abandoned in the woods, encountering a child-eating witch, and suffering neglect and abuse from their stepmother present considerable psychological stressors. Additionally, the loss of their mother at a young age represents a major traumatic event. As established by Brent and Melhem (2018) and Patten (1991), the early loss of a parent can increase vulnerability to depression. Osterweis et al. (1984) further assert that such losses during critical developmental stages leave children emotionally susceptible to various psychopathologies.

Given the severity and multiplicity of these adverse experiences, Hansel and Gretel might exhibit overlapping diagnoses, particularly major depressive disorder (MDD) and post-traumatic stress disorder (PTSD). However, in the case of Hansel and Gretel, it is likely that their PTSD symptoms would be pronounced due to the traumatic nature of their experiences. For example, triggers such as separation, the presence of a new maternal figure, or reminders related to food scarcity might evoke distressing memories and symptoms. These trauma-related issues and strategies for coping will be addressed further in the Intervention section.

The manifestation of MDD in children differs somewhat from that in adults. Typically, MDD is characterized by persistent sadness or loss of interest, impacting cognitive, behavioral, and physical functioning (Parritz & Troy, 2011). Episodes tend to be recurrent, lasting approximately seven to nine months. Hansel and Gretel's behavior in the story suggests depressive symptoms such as a sad or withdrawn mood—especially in the presence of their stepmother—somatic complaints, and anxiety, which may present as externalizing behaviors. Specific observed symptoms include a depressed affect, disinterest in age-appropriate activities, significant weight loss linked to famine, sleep disturbances driven by anxiety and fear, and fatigue from overwork in the witch's house.

However, other MDD symptoms such as psychomotor agitation, feelings of worthlessness or guilt, difficulty concentrating, and recurrent thoughts of death or suicidal ideation are not clearly depicted in the story.

To meet the diagnostic criteria for MDD, five or more symptoms must be present for at least two weeks, accompanied by impairment in age-appropriate functioning (Parritz & Troy, 2011). Additionally, research indicates that girls are twice as likely as boys to develop depression, placing Gretel at a heightened risk.

To ensure appropriate diagnosis and treatment, a comprehensive assessment of the children's symptoms is essential. Clinicians utilize multiple assessment tools to gain a holistic understanding, including self-report inventories, parental reports, medical examinations, and behavioral observations (Parritz & Troy, 2011). One well-established tool is the Children's Depression Inventory (Kovacs, 1978), which demonstrates strong reliability and validity (Saylor et al., 1984). Early and accurate diagnosis is critical, as untreated MDD can adversely affect developmental trajectories and result in ongoing struggles throughout adolescence and adulthood.

Etiology

Regarding comorbidity, Flory and Yehuda (2015) found that approximately half of individuals with PTSD also meet criteria for MDD. This overlap may be explained by shared symptoms between the two disorders or by the existence of a trauma-related phenotype representing their co-occurrence (Flory & Yehuda, 2015). Additionally, maltreatment significantly increases a child's vulnerability to developing depression (Parritz & Troy, 2011). The etiology of MDD is multifactorial, involving physiological, social, emotional, and environmental domains, as described by the multifactorial risk model. PTSD similarly arises from these interrelated factors.

Regarding heritability, some research suggests a genetic predisposition to MDD. However, the biological histories of Hansel and Gretel's parents remain unknown, leaving their genetic risk speculative. It is plausible that their father may suffer from depression, as depressive parents often have children who exhibit a range of internalizing and externalizing problems. Notably, physiological differences, particularly neurological, distinguish depressed individuals from those without depression (Parritz & Troy, 2011). Nonetheless, it remains challenging to determine whether these differences stem from genetic factors or are consequences of the disorder's onset.

Social and emotional factors also contribute to the onset of MDD in children. Specifically, the child's attachment to their caregivers shapes their emotional regulation, expression, and ability to form future relationships (Parritz & Troy, 2011). A secure attachment promotes healthier developmental outcomes. In this case, after the death of their biological mother, Hansel and Gretel's father remarried a woman who was neglectful and abusive, refusing to meet their basic needs, such as food and shelter. Although their father was loving, he was unable to manage the situation effectively, resulting in chronic stress for the children that further increased their vulnerability to depression.

Finally, the environment in which a child is raised plays a crucial role in the development of MDD. The absence of their biological mother affected the siblings' development, and their father's occupation as a woodcutter—a "poor man's" job in the story—limited the family's resources. Evidently, the children do not attend school, likely due to their socioeconomic status. Moreover, having to assist their father reduced opportunities for engaging in age-appropriate, pleasurable activities. Overall, poverty interacts with other risk factors, amplifying the likelihood of developing depression.

Treatment/Interventions

Intervention for Hansel and Gretel would require a comprehensive approach addressing symptoms of both PTSD and MDD. Initially, it is crucial to manage acute symptoms promptly, followed by sustained efforts to maintain long-term improvement.

For depression, pharmacological treatments target neurological pathways; however, there is debate about the appropriateness of medication use in children during critical developmental periods (Parritz & Troy, 2011). Research generally supports a more holistic approach that combines medication with psychotherapy. Cognitive-behavioral therapy (CBT) and interpersonal therapy (IPT)—which focus on relationship-centered techniques—have proven effective for children experiencing mood disorders like depression (Parritz & Troy, 2011). These therapies help children identify and understand their emotions and depressive symptoms, while encouraging engagement in enjoyable activities.

Including Hansel and Gretel's father in therapy sessions could strengthen their family bond and provide additional support. The father himself might benefit from individual therapy to improve his parenting skills and better support his children. Importantly, therapeutic interventions should align with the children's developmental stages, as transitions may present opportunities for greater receptivity to change and growth (Parritz & Troy, 2011).

Conclusion

The tale of Hansel and Gretel is both a compelling and harrowing story of survival and maturation. Despite facing numerous traumatic events at a young age, the siblings demonstrated remarkable resilience, primarily through mutual support and cooperation. Nonetheless, they remain vulnerable to developing PTSD and/or MDD. Effective interventions are available, including pharmacological treatments, CBT, and interpersonal therapy. Ultimately, involving their father in the therapeutic process is likely to be a crucial component for the family's healing and recovery.

References

Boyd, D. R., & Bee, H. L. (2019). *Lifespan development*. Pearson.

Brent, D., & Melhem, N. (2018, November 16). *In longest and most detailed study of paediatric grief following parental loss to date, department researchers find increased rates of depression and functional impairment*. University of Pittsburgh, Department of Psychiatry. https://www.psychiatry.pitt.edu/news/longest-and-most-detailed-study-pediatric-grief-following-parental-loss-date-department

Chiracu, A. (2016). Anxiety in children. *Romanian Journal of Cognitive-Behavioral Therapy and Hypnosis, 3*(2), 36–39. https://www.rjcbth.ro/image/data/v3-i2/V3I2_Alina%20Chiracu_RJCBTH.pdf

Erikson, E. H. (1963). Childhood and society (2nd ed.). New York: Norton.

Flory, J. D., & Yehuda, R. (2015). Comorbidity between post-traumatic stress disorder and major depressive disorder: Alternative explanations and treatment considerations. *Dialogues in Clinical Neuroscience, 17*(2), 141–150. https://doi.org/10.31887/DCNS.2015.17.2/jflory

Grimm, J., & Grimm, W. (2018). *Grimms' household fairy tales: The original 1812 collection*. Suzeteo Enterprises.

Hoffman, L. W. (2003). Methodological issues in the studies of SES, parenting, and child development. In M. H. Bornstein & R. H. Bradley (Eds.), *Socioeconomic status, parenting, and child development* (pp. 125–143). Lawrence Erlbaum Associates Publishers.

Jordan, W. C. (1996). *The great famine: Northern Europe in the early fourteenth century*. Princeton University Press.

Kovacs, M. (1978). *Children's depression inventory*. PsycTESTS Dataset. https://doi.org/10.1037/t00788-000

Miranda, M. C., Nóbrega, F. J., Sato, K., Pompéia, S., Sinnes, E. G., & Bueno, O. F. A. (2007). Neuropsychology and malnutrition: A study with 7 to 10 years-old children in a poor community. *Revista Brasileira de Saúde Materno Infantil, 7*(1), 45–54. https://www.scielo.br/j/rbsmi/a/7hjyMGRN4X4s7gzm4Hkzqbm/?lang=en&format=pdf

Osterweis, M., Solomon, F., & Green, M. (Eds.). (1984). Bereavement during childhood and adolescence. In *Bereavement: Reactions, consequences, and care*. Institute of Medicine (US) Committee for the Study of Health Consequences of the Stress of Bereavement. https://www.ncbi.nlm.nih.gov/books/NBK217849/

Parritz, R. H., & Troy, M. F. (2011). *Disorders of childhood: Development and psychopathology*. Wadsworth Cengage Learning.

Patten, S. B. (1991). The loss of a parent during childhood as a risk factor for depression. *The Canadian Journal of Psychiatry, 36*(10), 706–711. https://doi.org/10.1177/070674379103601002

Piaget, J., & Inhelder, B. (1969). *The psychology of the child*. Basic Books.

Roubinov, D. S., & Boyce, W. T. (2017). Parenting and SES: Relative values or enduring principles? *Current Opinion in Psychology, 15*, 162–167. https://doi.org/10.1016/j.copsyc.2017.03.001

Saylor, C. F., Finch, A. J., Spirito, A., & Bennett, B. (1984). The children's depression inventory: A systematic evaluation of psychometric properties. *Journal of Consulting and Clinical Psychology, 52*(6), 955–967. https://doi.org/10.1037/0022-006x.52.6.955

Stormshak, E. A., Bullock, B. M., & Falkenstein, C. A. (2009). Harnessing the power of sibling relationships as a tool for optimizing social-emotional development. *New Directions for Child and Adolescent Development, 2009*(126), 61–77. https://doi.org/10.1002/cd.257

CHAPTER 6

Peter Pan

Aikaterini Avgerinou and Anna Rombotis

Abstract This chapter explores the character of Peter Pan, known as the boy who never wanted to grow up, from the story written by J.M. Barrie in 1902. Peter Pan, who is kidnapped from his family, more specifically from his mother, experiences separation anxiety and distress from being away from his beloved family, even though his kidnapper entices him by telling him he will never get old now that he is away from his family. Peter Pan travels to Neverland, by flying in the sky with his miniature fairy to Neverland, a fantastic, magical island, where he is faced with outcasts and pirates fighting. Although Peter Pan's age is not defined, he is in middle childhood between six to twelve years of age, most seemingly nearing late childhood and early adolescence. His unique development will be assessed and diagnosed while taking into consideration his emotional, social, physical, and cognitive development. In this vignette, Peter Pan is diagnosed with disruptive attachment disorder, in early childhood and post-traumatic stress disorder (PTSD), in late childhood and early adolescence, and is assessed through evaluating his demographics, risk factors, protective factors, attachment style, etiology of the syndrome/disorder, and clinical treatment interventions.

A. Avgerinou (✉) • A. Rombotis
Hellenic American University Alumna, Athens, Greece
e-mail: aavgerinou@hauniv.edu; arombotis@hauniv.edu

A. Sax (ed.), *Understanding Child Psychopathology Through Fairytales*, https://doi.org/10.1007/978-3-032-14097-5_6

Keywords Middle childhood • Childhood trauma • Risk factors • Protective factors • Emotional regulation • Kidnapping • Disruptive attachment disorder • Post-traumatic stress • Post-traumatic stress disorder

The Story of Peter Pan

Peter Pan is widely known as the tale of a boy who never wanted to grow up. However, there are two sides to this narrative. The original story was introduced by J.M. Barrie in 1902 (Bauer & Lowne, 2020). It begins with a baby boy kidnapped from his family—specifically, from his mother. Before abducting the child, the kidnapper attempts to appear friendly and kind, weaving a story that the boy will never age once taken away. Despite the kidnapping, Peter remains a happy and cheerful boy, driven by the hope that his mother still waits and cares for him. Eventually, Peter decides to return to his mother, only to face rejection and disappointment when he discovers he has been replaced by a new baby boy (Fig. 6.1).

Barrie based his story on true events—his own brother died at age 14, and some elements were inspired by Barrie's mother (Bauer & Lowne, 2020). The tale continues with Peter traveling to London to take Wendy and her siblings to Neverland, hoping they will stay with him forever. The group encounters many challenges, including battles with pirates. After defeating them, Wendy and her siblings choose to return home, while Peter remains a boy in Neverland.

The story underwent many revisions before becoming the character recognized today by adults and children alike through Disney films and books. In the more familiar versions, little information is shared about Peter's past. The story begins in Neverland, where Peter Pan is the captain of the Lost Boys, who are like brothers forming a family with him. According to Bauer and Lowne (2020), the Lost Boys are children who fell out of their baby carriages when nurses were distracted.

Demographic Background

Peter's exact age remains uncertain. In Barrie's original 1902 publication, it is mentioned that Peter "has all of his baby teeth," suggesting he is quite young, as most children lose their baby teeth by age 12 at the latest

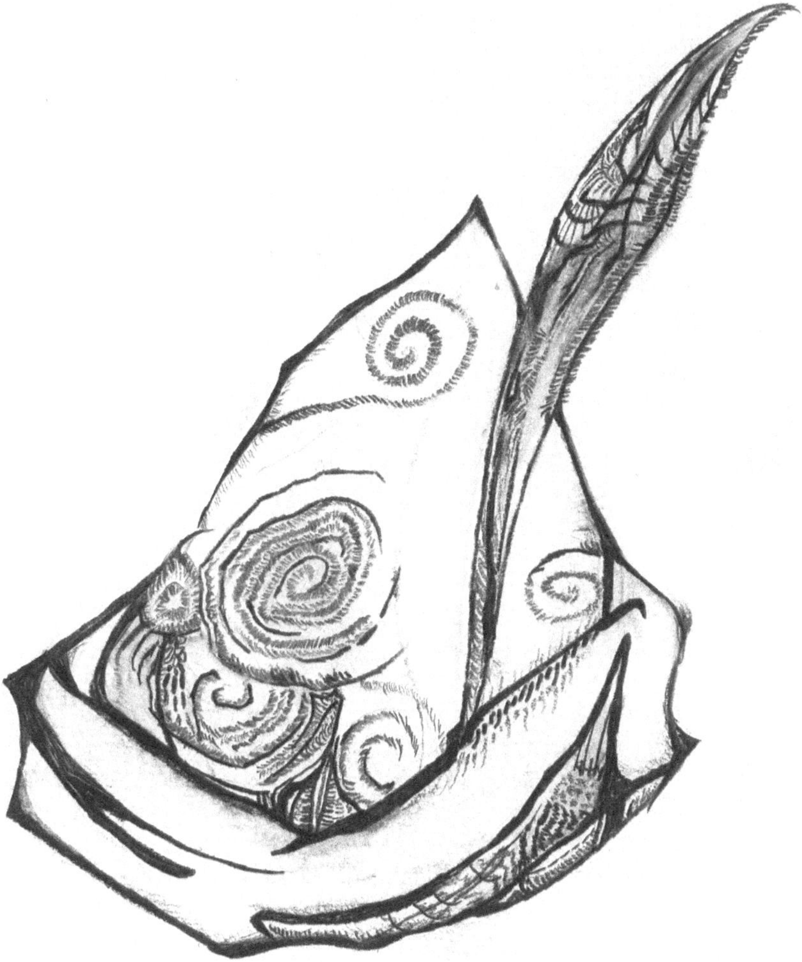

Fig. 6.1 Peter Pan

(Barclay, n.d.). Therefore, it can be inferred that Peter is in middle childhood, approximately between 6 and 12 years old, based on his linguistic abilities, motor skills, and general cognitive development.

Regarding his family background, it appears Peter only had a mother before going to live in Neverland, with his father absent. His English origin is implied, given his journey to London to collect Wendy and her siblings, which suggests he is likely Caucasian. Currently, he resides in Neverland alongside his fairy friend Tinker Bell, the Lost Boys, and a band of enemy pirates led by Captain Hook. He is typically depicted wearing leaves and other natural materials from the Earth. Across books, plays, and films, Peter appears healthy, lean, and agile. Notably, he has never attended any form of formal education.

Psychodynamic Analysis

Physically, Peter is often depicted as taller and more mature than the other children, reflecting his role as their leader in many books and films. He is agile, strong, and highly coordinated—able to fly (with the help of Tinker Bell's fairy dust), fend off pirates, and remain physically active. His healthy physique is consistently portrayed across various adaptations. Since Peter is perpetually stuck at a young age, it can be speculated that his neurological development has ceased. It is likely that he has developed selective attention skills, strong spatial perception and cognition, and an awareness of right and left orientation, while other areas such as executive functions may be underdeveloped (Boyd & Bee, 2019).

From a cognitive perspective, Peter is an intelligent child despite his persistent refusal to grow up and his seemingly "childish" behaviors. His linguistic abilities are advanced for his apparent age, as he speaks with few, if any, grammar or pronunciation errors. Given that he has lived far longer than his physical appearance suggests, it is reasonable to assume he has developed cognitive functions beyond those typical of his peers. He demonstrates the capacity to plan and think logically, skills necessary to survive in Neverland and to protect himself and his friends from the dangers posed by pirates.

According to psychodynamic theory, the latency stage begins around age six and continues until puberty (Boyd & Bee, 2019). This stage is significant for the development of the superego, which attempts to regulate desires arising from the id. Freud described the latency period as a transitional phase where the child remains caught between childhood and adolescence (Judge, 2013). It appears that Peter Pan is unable to move beyond this stage, with Neverland functioning as a space that enables his psychological stasis.

Socially, children in the latency stage begin to identify with different age groups and develop interpersonal relationships. Peter appears to maintain positive bonds with the Lost Boys as well as Wendy and her siblings. He also exhibits strong leadership skills as their captain. However, his relationship with adults is marked by aggression and avoidance; he rejects any form of communication or connection with them. Typically, at this developmental stage, physical aggression decreases while verbal aggression increases. With Peter, both forms of aggression are evident, especially when defending himself against adult figures. This behavior diverges from typical development, as preteens generally form stronger attachments to adult figures (Boyd & Bee, 2019).

Regarding emotional development, Peter displays notable traits—most prominently, his refusal to grow up. He views adults as the antagonists in his story, which fuels his desire to protect himself from them. He struggles with emotional regulation, expressing hurt, anger, and distrust toward adults—responses that are atypical for a child at his developmental stage.

Risk Factors

In Peter Pan's case, several risk factors contribute to his atypical development. Risk factors typically stem from one's family, environment, and broader social and economic context (Parritz & Troy, 2011). Peter's family background appears to have played a significant role in shaping his psychological state. While limited information is provided about his upbringing, it can be inferred that his mother was initially loving and nurturing, as Peter's longing to reunite with her suggests a secure early attachment. However, upon returning home and discovering that his mother had given birth to another child, Peter experienced feelings of rejection, replacement, and disappointment. This emotional trauma likely influenced his decision to remain a child forever, distancing himself from adults whom he perceives as sources of hurt and betrayal.

The absence of consistent adult caregiving figures deprives Peter of the security, guidance, and emotional support essential for healthy development. His persistent inability to self-regulate negative emotions toward adults is another notable risk factor. Furthermore, Peter's lack of formal education hinders his cognitive, social, and emotional growth, limiting his ability to adapt to typical developmental milestones. Financial instability is implied through his attire of leaves and natural materials, suggesting he lacks basic resources or means of self-sufficiency. Finally, his living environment is fraught with danger, as the constant threat of Captain Hook, his crew of pirates, and even the crocodile exposes Peter to potential physical harm or death.

Protective Factors

Despite these risks, several protective factors serve as buffers in Peter's life. He appears to have a naturally positive temperament, particularly evident in his interactions with peers. His close relationships with Wendy, the Lost Boys, and Tinker Bell provide him with a sense of companionship, belonging, and emotional support that partially compensates for the absence of traditional family figures. However, the limited number of protective factors in Peter's environment leaves him vulnerable to negative psychological and developmental outcomes in the long term.

Attachment Style

Peter Pan's attachment development deviates significantly from that of most children, largely due to his choice—or perhaps emotional need—to remain perpetually young. Attachment bonds typically begin in infancy and strengthen over time as the child builds secure relationships with their caregivers (Boyd & Bee, 2019). In Peter's case, the absence of a father figure from the very beginning creates an incomplete foundation for attachment formation. According to Bowlby's attachment theory, secure attachments are fostered through warm, nurturing, and consistent caregiving, which is essential for healthy emotional development (as cited in Brown et al., 2012). The lack of a paternal presence therefore leaves a gap in Peter's early attachment experience.

While it is implied that Peter initially shared a loving bond with his mother, this connection was disrupted when he was taken away from her at a very young age. Disrupted attachment occurs when a primary caregiver is no longer present in a child's life, leading to feelings of emotional detachment and insecurity (Schuengel et al., 2009). Peter's emotional trajectory reflects this: he grows increasingly mistrustful, defensive, and even hostile toward adult figures. The grief stemming from his perceived abandonment is compounded when, upon attempting to reunite with his mother, he discovers she has replaced him with another child. This perceived rejection becomes a pivotal emotional wound, influencing his vow never to return and his subsequent decision to avoid growing up altogether (Parritz & Troy, 2011).

From a Freudian perspective, Peter appears to be fixated in the Oedipus complex stage (Boyd & Bee, 2019). His intense hostility toward Captain Hook may be understood as a displaced expression of unresolved paternal conflict, as Hook symbolically represents the father figure Peter never had—or perhaps one he subconsciously resents for abandoning him. Additionally, Peter's protective and possessive attitude toward Wendy suggests that he perceives her as a surrogate mother figure. When Captain Hook kidnaps Wendy, Peter's world is momentarily shattered, echoing his earlier trauma of losing his real mother for a second time. This dynamic underscores how his disrupted attachment history continues to shape his emotional responses and relationships.

Diagnosis and Assessment

As previously discussed, Peter Pan appears to suffer from a disruptive attachment, a condition that can lead to a variety of negative developmental outcomes and increase the risk of psychopathology later in life. Bowlby (1963) emphasized that the formation of a secure attachment in early childhood is a strong predictor of positive emotional, cognitive, and behavioral development. Conversely, disruptions in attachment can impair a child's ability to regulate emotions, develop healthy relationships, and engage effectively in learning (Parritz & Troy, 2011).

Peter's lack of a stable parental caregiver has left him vulnerable in these areas. His repeated displays of aggression, anger, and mistrust toward adults suggest difficulties with self-regulation. Schore (2002) links early attachment experiences to right-brain development, which is crucial for emotional regulation and bodily self-control. When attachment is insecure or disrupted, this development can be compromised, leaving the individual prone to emotional dysregulation. In Peter's case, the energy he spends attempting to manage his negative emotions may hinder his growth in other developmental domains (Schore, 2002).

This disruption appears to have profoundly impacted Peter's sense of self and understanding of the world (Parritz & Troy, 2011). His choice to live in Neverland—a fantastical world detached from reality—can be seen as a coping mechanism to avoid the responsibilities, challenges, and painful emotions associated with growing up. This pattern of behavior has been popularly described as Peter Pan Syndrome in pop psychology, referring to adults who resist maturity, avoid responsibility, and display emotional unavailability (Raypole, 2020). Although not recognized as a formal diagnosis in the DSM-5, it captures aspects of Peter's personality and coping strategies. Additionally, the early trauma of being separated from his mother during a critical developmental stage may have left Peter vulnerable to post-traumatic stress (PTS) symptoms or potentially post-traumatic stress disorder (PTSD).

Several assessment methods could help identify attachment disruptions in Peter's case. A thorough review of his early family history, combined with clinical observations of his behaviors, would likely highlight signs of insecure attachment. Established tools such as Ainsworth's Maternal Sensitivity Scale, the CARE-Index, and the Maternal Behavior Q-Sort are commonly used to assess attachment difficulties (National Collaborating Centre for Mental Health, 2015). However, these tools are designed for use with a child's caregiver, which is not possible in Peter's situation. Instead, detailed behavioral observations and carefully structured clinical interviews—possibly conducted in the presence of a trusted peer to help Peter feel safe—would be more appropriate. It is important to note that diagnosing specific attachment disorders becomes increasingly complex as a child grows older, since symptoms such as aggression, anxiety, and depression can arise from a variety of etiological pathways, not solely from attachment-related difficulties (Parritz & Troy, 2011).

Etiology

The etiology of attachment disorders is typically understood as a dynamic interaction between the characteristics of both the caregiver and the child. Parental factors, such as the presence of mental illness or an inability to provide consistent care, are well-established contributors. In Peter's case, little is known about his mother's mental state or parenting style, making it difficult to determine her specific role in the disruption of their bond.

However, observations of Peter himself provide insight into possible contributing factors. He is described as having an active, impulsive, excitable, and sometimes aggressive temperament. Research suggests that temperament compatibility between a child and caregiver facilitates secure attachment, while mismatched temperaments can create tension and difficulty in forming healthy bonds (Kaya et al., 2020). It is possible that even before their separation, differences in temperament may have complicated Peter's attachment to his mother.

Furthermore, the trauma of being physically separated from his primary caregiver at a sensitive age appears to have left lasting emotional scars. Combined with environmental instability, the absence of parental support, and his own challenging temperament, these factors contribute to Peter's disrupted attachment. Cognitive distortions, such as his belief that adults are inherently harmful or untrustworthy, further reinforce his decision to isolate himself in Neverland and avoid growing up altogether. Collectively, these biological, psychological, and environmental influences help explain the etiology of Peter's maladaptive attachment patterns.

Treatment/Interventions

Interventions for Peter Pan should primarily address the significant stressors and emotional challenges stemming from his disrupted attachment. Child-centered play therapy (CCPT) has been shown to be an effective approach in helping children rebuild a sense of security and trust toward adult caregivers (Landreth, 2012). Through non-directive play therapy sessions, Peter could gradually express and process his underlying fears, anger, and feelings of abandonment in a safe, supportive environment. CCPT could help him develop healthier emotional regulation skills while fostering a more positive view of adult figures.

If Peter were to be reintroduced to the real world and reunited with his mother, a more integrative approach involving filial therapy would be highly beneficial. Filial therapy encourages active parental involvement in the therapeutic process, allowing parents to learn play-based techniques to strengthen their bond with their child (Geurney, 1983). Since children's behaviors often reflect their home environment, addressing the parent–child relationship directly is crucial to achieving lasting change.

In this process, Peter's mother would first meet with the child therapist for an introductory session, then observe CCPT in practice. She would receive training, engage in supervised sessions, and eventually conduct play sessions independently (Geurney, 1983). The therapeutic goals would include improving her ability to acknowledge Peter's feelings, set consistent boundaries, empathize with his emotional reactions, and rebuild trust. While reuniting mother and son after prolonged separation would likely be emotionally challenging, educating Peter's mother on the potential benefits of this intervention may increase her willingness to engage. A systemic approach, in which the therapist, supervisor, and caregiver collaborate closely, can further enhance outcomes for Peter's long-term development (Cochran & Cochran, 2017).

Conclusion

Peter Pan's story, while fantastical, reflects a psychological portrait of a boy struggling with the emotional consequences of early attachment trauma. His choice to remain in Neverland, refusing to grow up, symbolizes his attempt to escape the pain of abandonment and avoid the perceived dangers of adulthood. The disruption of his bond with his primary caregiver—exacerbated by the emotional wound of feeling replaced by another child—has left Peter mistrustful of adults, prone to anger and defensiveness, and emotionally arrested in his development.

Despite these challenges, Peter possesses notable protective factors, including strong friendships with the Lost Boys, Wendy, and Tinker Bell, which provide him with social support and some sense of belonging. However, these compensatory relationships cannot fully substitute for the secure attachment he lost. Without intervention, Peter remains at risk of further emotional dysregulation and the development of more entrenched psychopathological patterns over time.

Therapeutic interventions such as CCPT and filial therapy offer a pathway toward healing. By fostering emotional expression, rebuilding trust, and re-establishing a nurturing bond with his mother, Peter may eventually learn to process his trauma, regulate his emotions, and accept the challenges and responsibilities that come with growing up. While difficult, this process could allow Peter to achieve healthier developmental outcomes and a more secure sense of self.

References

Barclay, S. (n.d.). A character analysis of Peter Pan. *Cracked Spines*. http://crackedspine.blogspot.com/2014/01/a-character-analysis-of-peter-pan.html

Bauer, P., & Lowne, C. (2020). Peter Pan|plot, analysis, characters, & facts. *Encyclopedia Britannica*. https://www.britannica.com/topic/Peter-Pan-play-by-Barrie

Bowlby, J. (1963). Pathological mourning and childhood mourning. *Journal of the American Psychoanalytic Association, 11*(3), 500–541. https://doi.org/10.1177/000306516301100303

Boyd, D. R., & Bee, H. L. (2019). *Lifespan development*. Pearson.

Brown, G. L., Mangelsdorf, S. C., & Neff, C. (2012). Father involvement, paternal sensitivity, and father–child attachment security in the first 3 years. *Journal of Family Psychology, 26*(3), 421–430. https://doi.org/10.1037/a0027836

Cochran, J. L., & Cochran, N. H. (2017). Effects of child-centered play therapy for students with highly-disruptive behavior in high-poverty schools. *International Journal of Play Therapy, 26*(2), 59–72. https://doi.org/10.1037/pla0000052

Geurney, L. (1983, April). *Play therapy conference.* Conference held at North Texas State University, Denton.

Judge, B. (2013). *Analysis: Peter Pan.* English 353 Children's Literature. https://6450055952l8429375.weebly.com/analysis-peter-pan.html

Kaya, İ., Seven, S., & Ildız, G. İ. (2020). The contributions of temperament characteristics to attachment in 6-year-old children. *International Education Studies, 13*(7), 156. https://doi.org/10.5539/ies.v13n7p156

Landreth, G. L. (2012). *Play therapy: The art of the relationship.* Routledge.

National Collaborating Centre for Mental Health (UK). (2015). *Children's attachment: Attachment in children and young people who are adopted from care, in care or at high risk of going into care.* National Institute for Health and Care Excellence (NICE; NICE Guideline, No. 26.) 8, Identification and assessment of attachment difficulties. https://www.ncbi.nlm.nih.gov/books/NBK356194/?report=classic

Parritz, R. H., & Troy, M. F. (2011). *Disorders of childhood: Development and psychopathology.* Wadsworth Cengage Learning.

Raypole, C. (2020, March 19). Peter Pan syndrome: When people just can't grow up. *Healthline.* https://www.healthline.com/health/peter-pan-syndrome#narcissism

Schore, A. N. (2002). Advances in neuropsychoanalysis, attachment theory, and trauma research: Implications for self psychology. *Psychoanalytic Inquiry, 22*(3), 433–484. https://doi.org/10.1080/07351692209348996

Schuengel, C., Oosterman, M., & Sterkenburg, P. S. (2009). Children with disrupted attachment histories: Interventions and psychophysiological indices of effects. *Child and Adolescent Psychiatry and Mental Health, 3*(1), 26. https://doi.org/10.1186/1753-2000-3-26

CHAPTER 7

The Little Mermaid: Ariel

Sara Eleni Pliacha and Anna Rombotis

Abstract The Little Mermaid, written by Hans Christian Andersen (*The little mermaid*. C. A. Reitzel, 1837), is the tale of a mermaid princess named Ariel, the youngest of six daughters of the Sea King. After losing her mother at a young age, Ariel was raised by her grandmother. In the story, Ariel is fifteen years old. It is apparent that she belongs to a royal family, whereby her father is deemed the "Sea King," making her a princess. Thus, it can be assumed that she is supported financially by her father and holds a high status in society. Ariel longs to be human and live among them. She spends long hours of the day, observing humans on a boat. After severe weather conditions, the boat catches on fire, and she saves the prince she has fantasized about meeting. Unfortunately, Ariel self-harms by giving up her tongue for human legs to be with the prince. Her dark journey ends with her taking her own life, as she is consumed by suffering, knowing that the prince never loved her during the time she spent with him. Her unique development will be assessed and diagnosed while taking

S. E. Pliacha (✉) • A. Rombotis
Hellenic American University Alumna, Athens, Greece
e-mail: spliacha@hauniv.edu; arombotis@hauniv.edu

A. Sax (ed.), *Understanding Child Psychopathology Through Fairytales*, https://doi.org/10.1007/978-3-032-14097-5_7

into consideration her emotional, social, physical, and cognitive development. In this vignette, Ariel is diagnosed with reactive attachment disorder in infancy and BD-I in adolescence, and is assessed through evaluating her demographics, risk factors, protective factors, attachment style, etiology of the syndrome, and clinical treatment interventions.

Keywords Adolescence • Identity development • Loss • Unfulfilled love • Self-harm • Risk factors • Protective factors • Reactive attachment disorder • Bipolar disorder-I

The Story of Ariel

The Little Mermaid by Hans Christian Andersen (1837) tells the tragic tale of Ariel, the youngest of six daughters of the Sea King. After losing her mother at a young age, Ariel is raised by her grandmother. She is described as "a beautiful young girl with the sweetest voice in the kingdom" (Andersen, 1837). From early on, Ariel is fascinated by humans and the world above the sea, spending years dreaming of experiencing it for herself. On her fifteenth birthday, she finally gets the chance to glimpse this other world. While observing a ship celebrating a party, a storm strikes, lightning sets the ship ablaze, and Ariel courageously saves a prince from drowning. Captivated by him, she becomes obsessed, often visiting the seashore to watch him from afar (Fig. 7.1).

Unable to contain her longing, Ariel seeks out a sea witch, sacrificing her voice—having her tongue cut out—in exchange for legs to live among humans. Despite finding her prince on land, he does not return her love. Instead, he calls her his "dumb foundling" and makes her sleep on the floor beside his bed. When the prince later chooses to marry another princess, Ariel faces the choice of killing him to return home or sacrificing herself. Consumed by love, she chooses death, throwing herself into the sea.

Demographic Background

In Andersen's story, Ariel is a 15-year-old teenager belonging to a royal family, as her father is the "Sea King," making her a princess. This status suggests that she has been well provided for financially and enjoys a

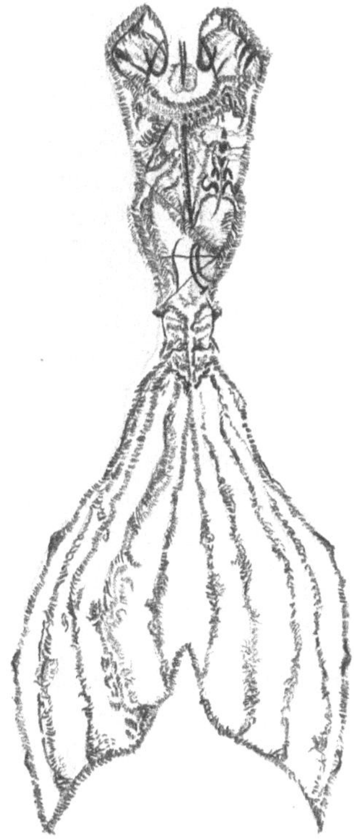

Fig. 7.1 The Little Mermaid-Ariel

privileged position in her society. Ariel is described as having white skin, indicating a Caucasian racial background.

After the loss of her mother, Ariel was raised primarily by her grandmother, alongside her six older sisters, though their relationships are not explored in depth. While Ariel's material needs were met, the absence of her mother may have disrupted the formation of a secure attachment during childhood, potentially shaping her emotional development and later vulnerability in relationships.

Psychodynamic Analysis

Focusing on Ariel's physical development, it is believed that she is reaching many milestones within this domain. At the age of 15, she holds excellent gross motor and fine motor skills, apparent through her ability to swim long distances and even save a prince from drowning by returning him safely to the seashore. Despite these abilities, she seems unhappy in her current body and wishes she could alter it to be accepted and loved by the prince. This leads her to seeking out the sea witch who proposes to cut out her tongue in exchange for legs.

Ariel's social development is lacking due to her isolation and lack of knowledge about the culture of the princes' world. She is aware that life in the human world is different from her own, and her knowledge of their world comes from the stories told by her family members. Not having the opportunity to form connections with individuals outside of her immediate family could have a negative effect on Ariel's social development. Falling in love with the prince and willing to run away to learn more about him could have been a result of loneliness. Boyd and Bee (2019) suggest that teenagers lack some ability to emotionally regulate themselves, whereby engaging in risky behaviors due to low impulse control and a lack of healthy coping mechanisms.

In observance of Erikson's stages of psychosocial development from birth to 11 years old, Ariel went through the Trust versus Mistrust stage in a healthy way as she learned to trust her family members and seek them when needed (Erikson, 1963). She also grew to be quite autonomous, as she drifted further away from her family's microculture and expectations. This is evident when she begins to question her surroundings and compares all she knows to the prince and his world. The Industry versus Inferiority stage pertains to an individual's competence versus feelings of inferiority. In the story, Ariel is repeatedly told by her grandmother that if she is not loved by someone, she will not go to heaven when she dies (Andersen, 1837). In response to this, Ariel runs away from home, allows a sea witch to cut out her tongue in exchange for legs, resulting in excruciating pain, and loses her tail, all to save her soul after death. Although she appears competent, this event leads to problems in the next stage of Identity versus Role Confusion, between the ages of 12 to 18 years old. Given that Ariel eventually turns her back on her community and trades it all to be with the man she loves, it can be speculated that she is stuck in the role confusion stage and never developed her own identity. Cognitively, such unresolved internal conflicts could have led her to see the prince's love as her only path to identity and self-worth. As a result, this possibly limited her problem-solving abilities and increased her vulnerability toward making self-destructive choices.

Ariel's emotional world reflects an insecure attachment stemming from her grandmother's caregiving approach. Ariel and her sisters were raised in an isolated environment by their grandmother. She had an authoritarian style of parenting and strong beliefs about how royalty should behave, which she instilled in her granddaughters. The authoritarian parenting style is characterized by low degrees of nurturance and communication toward the child, whereby caregivers exert more control over their children and have high expectations (Boyd & Bee, 2019; Baumrind, 1966). We see this in her grandmother's parenting style as she chooses to punish Ariel with the oyster shells clamping down on their tails to show they are royal. Her harsh upbringing could have contributed to Ariel's unstable emotional state and her impulsive decisions in search of love and validation from others, especially the prince.

Risk Factors

Ariel faced multiple risk factors that may have contributed to her eventual suicide. Raised in an isolated environment under the strict rule of her authoritarian grandmother, she was subjected from an early age to expectations centered on superficial values—namely, her royal status and the pressure to secure a husband. These external demands likely undermined her self-worth and contributed to low self-esteem.

Her relationship with her primary caregiver reflects an insecure-avoidant attachment style (Ainsworth et al., 1978), shaped by her grandmother's lack of nurturance and her father's emotional neglect. As noted by Boyd and Bee (2019), insecure-avoidant attachment develops in infancy when a child avoids seeking comfort from their caregiver and shows little preference for them over others, setting the stage for difficulties in forming healthy relationships later in life.

Li and Hu (2023) emphasize that a child's social and emotional development depends on positive connections with competent adults, supportive peer groups, access to education, and opportunities for social interaction. Ariel was deprived of these experiences. She and her sisters were isolated from peers their age and had little exposure to social activities outside of family life. This lack of healthy relationships and external support networks likely hindered her ability to regulate emotions and cope with stress, making her more vulnerable to despair and suicidal behavior.

Protective Factors

Despite her tragic outcome, Ariel demonstrates notable personal resilience. Her decision to endure immense pain and sacrifice her voice in exchange for legs, while arguably reckless, reflects her courage, curiosity, and determination to experience a life beyond the confines of her upbringing.

However, this act can also be interpreted symbolically, illustrating Ariel's powerlessness and inability to express her true self. Having grown up in an environment where her value was tied to approval and external validation, she lacked an authentic sense of identity. The presence of a supportive, understanding figure outside her authoritarian family structure may have helped her develop healthier coping strategies and ultimately altered her fate.

Attachment Style

Attachment styles are shaped by a combination of factors from birth through childhood, including temperament, parenting style, and protective environmental influences. Research by Gross et al. (2017) highlights that secure attachment to caregivers fosters prosocial behavior and emotional stability when children begin forming relationships outside their families. In contrast, insecure attachment—particularly the avoidant type—can lead to difficulties coping with stress, reluctance to seek help, and withdrawal from others (Ainsworth et al., 1978).

Ariel demonstrates many signs of insecure-avoidant attachment. From an early age, she internalized her pain, often isolating herself even from her sisters and grandmother. Year after year, as her older sisters ventured to the surface on their birthdays, Ariel remained behind, quietly longing for connection yet unable to express her feelings. Later, when she meets the prince, she again suffers in silence, obsessing over him but confiding in no one. This pattern of emotional suppression and withdrawal suggests a deep-seated inability to rely on others for comfort, likely stemming from a lack of nurturing and secure bonds in childhood.

Diagnosis and Assessment

Reactive Attachment Disorder (RAD) is characterized by inhibited emotional responses, including a lack of seeking comfort from caregivers in times of distress. According to DSM-5 criteria, the inhibited subtype of RAD presents as persistent social and emotional disturbances, such as minimal responsiveness to others (APA, 2013). Ariel demonstrates several features consistent with this diagnosis: as she grows older, she increasingly isolates herself and displays episodes of unexplained sadness or fearfulness. Her upbringing involved social neglect and a lack of affection, with her grandmother portrayed as a cold, authoritarian figure rather than a nurturing caregiver. Additionally, early loss of her mother and neglect by her father represent significant disruptions in her primary attachments, both of which are risk factors for RAD.

Difficulties in attachment can also impede the development of a stable sense of self during adolescence—a stage marked by rapid physical, emotional, and social changes. According to Erikson (1968), achieving a cohesive identity is the primary developmental task of adolescence, laying the foundation for future intimacy and healthy relationships. When psychopathology interferes with this process, as it appears to in Ariel's case, it can lead to a negative self-perception and an increased risk of mood disorders (Parritz & Troy, 2011). Research supports a link between insecure attachment and mood disorders (Herstell et al., 2021), and Alston (2001) suggests a possible correlation between RAD and Bipolar I disorder (BD).

Bipolar I disorder is characterized by alternating manic and depressive episodes, which Ariel appears to exhibit (Parritz & Troy, 2011). Among adolescents, manic phases may include grandiose delusions, hyperactivity during nighttime hours, hypersexuality, and risk-taking behaviors. These symptoms can shift rapidly within hours or days. Notably, suicidal tendencies are a serious concern in BD, particularly among adolescent girls who report suicidal ideation more frequently than boys (Parritz & Troy, 2011). Ariel's self-harming act of removing her tongue could be understood as an impulsive, risk-taking behavior associated with a manic state, possibly fueled by delusions that the prince was in love with her.

Diagnosing BD in children and adolescents is particularly challenging, as symptoms often overlap with those of anxiety, ADHD, personality disorders, and substance use (Parritz & Troy, 2011). While the clinical presentation of BD is similar in adults and adolescents, it is more frequently misdiagnosed in the latter (Youngstrom et al., 2009). Tools such as the

Child Bipolar Questionnaire (Papolos et al., 2006) can help screen for early signs, but accurate diagnosis requires comprehensive evaluation, including self-reports, parent and teacher reports, medical assessments, and behavioral observations.

At present, no validated instrument exists for diagnosing RAD specifically. Children with histories of adoption, abuse, foster care, or institutional living should be referred to a child psychologist or psychiatrist for thorough biopsychosocial assessment (Ellis et al., 2023). Such assessments should track attachment behaviors over time, observing key markers of secure attachment—such as seeking comfort, maintaining eye contact, and initiating interaction—to guide early intervention.

Etiology

The development of RAD is strongly associated with early experiences of neglect and lack of affection from caregivers. Ariel's grandmother is portrayed as emotionally cold and authoritarian, failing to provide the warmth and security necessary for healthy attachment. Research indicates that childhood abuse and neglect can alter brain development, impacting working memory, executive functioning, and structures such as the left cerebral hemisphere and hippocampus (Ellis et al., 2023). As a result, children with RAD often struggle with social skills, experience rejection from adults and peers, develop a negative self-image, and exhibit psychosomatic distress. In Ariel's case, isolation, absence of friendships, and lack of positive family relationships likely contributed to her risky behaviors and desperation to alter her physical self for acceptance.

Genetic factors also influence vulnerability to BD. Children with a familial history of bipolar disorder may have a heightened predisposition, though parents with the disorder may fail to recognize symptoms, while unaffected parents may dismiss them as typical adolescence (Youngstrom et al., 2009). Other contributing factors include disrupted sleep patterns, compromised executive functioning, and exposure to stressful life events (Parritz & Troy, 2011). Although it is unclear whether Ariel inherited a genetic predisposition, her emotionally deprived upbringing could have acted as a trigger for latent BD symptoms.

Additional risk factors for suicidality in adolescence include early puberty, mood and adjustment disorders, identity struggles, low self-esteem, and profound hopelessness (Erikson, 1963; Parritz & Troy, 2011). Ariel's inability to express emotional pain or seek support likely intensified her internal suffering. Ultimately, the interplay of insecure attachment, possible genetic vulnerability, environmental stressors, and identity confusion contributed to her tragic decision to end her life.

Treatment/Interventions

Effective treatment of RAD requires a comprehensive approach involving both the child and caregivers. According to Ellis et al. (2023), intervention strategies should emphasize parent education and trauma-focused therapy. Parent education aims to equip caregivers with positive, non-punitive behavior management strategies, improved understanding of nonverbal communication, and the ability to identify and manage triggers. Parent-child psychotherapy fosters bonding, empathy, and trust, helping repair disrupted attachment patterns and enabling the child to develop healthy emotional regulation.

The treatment of bipolar disorder (BD) in children and adolescents focuses on three primary goals: (1) managing acute symptoms, (2) maintaining improvements over time, and (3) addressing long-term complications, such as suicidality, while supporting overall growth and development. Many young individuals with BD seek treatment in outpatient settings (Kafantaris, 1995). Pharmacological intervention often involves mood stabilizers, with lithium being the most widely used and effective. For cases unresponsive to a single medication, a combination of drugs may be prescribed (Goldstein et al., 2012). However, caution is advised due to the ongoing neurological development in this age group.

Psychosocial therapies complement pharmacological treatment, offering significant benefits for both depression and bipolar disorder. Psychoeducation for families plays a crucial role in improving understanding of the illness, promoting adherence to treatment, and fostering a supportive home environment (Miklowitz et al., 2004; Goldstein et al., 2012). Long-term maintenance, with active family involvement, is essential for reducing relapse risk and supporting emotional and social development.

Conclusion

Princess Ariel's tragic fate appears to stem from multiple interwoven factors, particularly her emotionally deprived and unstable familial environment. From an early age, she lacked consistent warmth, security, and nurturing attachment figures. Her grandmother's authoritarian parenting style compounded her feelings of isolation and inadequacy, pushing Ariel to seek belonging in unfamiliar and ultimately harmful ways.

Her final decision—to embrace death rather than return home or harm the prince—reflects profound emotional dysregulation and cognitive distress. This choice highlights not only the depth of her internal struggle but also the absence of protective factors that might have supported healthier coping mechanisms. Ariel's desperate actions, from sacrificing her voice to seeking external validation of her worth, reveal the psychological toll of neglect and insecure attachment.

Children raised in nurturing, stable environments typically develop resilience, better decision-making skills, and an ability to navigate adversity safely. Ariel's story underscores the critical role of healthy caregiver relationships and early intervention in preventing maladaptive coping, severe mood disturbances, and, ultimately, tragic outcomes. Her narrative serves as a stark reminder of the long-lasting consequences of childhood neglect and unaddressed psychopathology.

References

Ainsworth, M. D. S., Blehar, M., Waters, E., & Wall, S. (1978). *Patterns of attachment.* Erlbaum.

Alston, J. F. (2001). Correlation between childhood bipolar I disorder and reactive attachment disorder, disinhibited type. In T. M. Levy (Ed.), *Handbook of attachment interventions* (2nd ed., pp. 193–242). Academic Press. https://doi.org/10.1016/B978012445860-4/50009-5

American Psychiatric Association. (2013). *Diagnostic and statistical manual of mental disorders* (5th ed.). American Psychiatric Association.

Andersen, H. C. (1837). *The little mermaid.* C. A. Reitzel.

Baumrind, D. (1966). Effects of authoritative parental control on child behaviour. *Child Development, 37*, 887–907. https://doi.org/10.2307/1126611

Boyd, D. R., & Bee, H. L. (2019). *Lifespan development.* Pearson.

Ellis, E. E., Yilanli, M., & Saadabadi, A. (2023, May 1). Reactive attachment disorder. In *StatPearls* [Internet]. StatPearls Publishing. https://www.ncbi.nlm.nih.gov/books/NBK537155/

Erikson, E. H. (1963). *Childhood and society* (2nd ed.). Norton.

Erikson, E. H. (1968). *Identity: Youth and crisis.* Norton & Co..

Goldstein, B. I., Sassi, R., & Diler, R. S. (2012). Pharmacologic treatment of bipolar disorder in children and adolescents. *Child and Adolescent Psychiatric*

Clinics of North America, 21(4), 911–939. https://doi.org/10.1016/j.chc.2012.07.004
Gross, J. T., Stern, J. A., Brett, B. E., & Cassidy, J. (2017). The multifaceted nature of prosocial behaviour in children: Links with attachment theory and research. *Social Development, 26*(4), 661–678. https://doi.org/10.1111/sode.12242
Herstell, S., Betz, L. T., Penzel, N., Chechelnizki, R., Filihagh, L., Antonucci, L., & Kambeitz, J. (2021). Insecure attachment as a transdiagnostic risk factor for major psychiatric conditions: A meta-analysis in bipolar disorder, depression and schizophrenia spectrum disorder. *Journal of Psychiatric Research, 144*, 190–201. https://doi.org/10.1016/j.jpsychires.2021.10.002
Kafantaris, V. (1995). Treatment of bipolar disorder in children and adolescents. *Journal of the American Academy of Child & Adolescent Psychiatry, 34*(6), 732–741. https://doi.org/10.1097/00004583-199506000-00013
Li, Q., & Hu, G. (2023). Positive impacts of perceived social support on prosocial behavior: The chain mediating role of moral identity and moral sensitivity. *Frontiers in Psychology, 14*, 1234977. https://doi.org/10.3389/fpsyg.2023.1234977
Miklowitz, D. J., George, E. L., Axelson, D. A., Kim, E. Y., Birmaher, B., Schneck, C., & Brent, D. A. (2004). Family-focused treatment for adolescents with bipolar disorder. *Journal of Affective Disorders, 82*, S113–S128. https://doi.org/10.1016/j.jad.2004.05.020
Papolos, D., Hennen, J., Cockerham, M. S., Thode, H. C., & Youngstrom, E. A. (2006). The child bipolar questionnaire: A dimensional approach to screening for pediatric bipolar disorder. *Journal of Affective Disorders, 95*(1–3), 149–158. https://doi.org/10.1016/j.jad.2006.03.026
Parritz, R. H., & Troy, M. F. (2011). *Disorders of childhood: Development and psychopathology*. Wadsworth Cengage Learning.
Youngstrom, E. A., Freeman, A. J., & Jenkins, M. M. (2009). The assessment of children and adolescents with bipolar disorder. *Child and Adolescent Psychiatric Clinics of North America, 18*(2), 353–390. https://doi.org/10.1016/j.chc.2008.12.002

CHAPTER 8

Robin Hood

Ioulia Fatourou and Anna Rombotis

Abstract The tale of Robin Hood, a figure renowned for redistributing wealth from the affluent to the impoverished, has its origins in tales dating back to the twelfth century. In Pyle's (*Some merry adventures of Robin Hood of great renown in Nottinghamshire*. F. Watts, 1967) published work, Robin Hood is depicted as a heroic figure championing the cause of social equality. Robin Hood wins an archery contest, subsequently kills a man in self-defense, and flees his homeland to evade being captured by the law. Throughout his journey, he recruits individuals to his side with the shared objective of taking from the wealthy and aiding the less fortunate. Although Robin Hood's exact age is not mentioned in the tale, it is assumed that he is in mid-adolescence, between fifteen and sixteen years of age. His unique development will be assessed and diagnosed while taking into consideration his emotional, social, physical, and cognitive development. In this vignette, Robin Hood is diagnosed with conduct disorder and is assessed through evaluating his demographics, risk factors, protective factors, attachment style, etiology of the syndrome/disorder, and clinical treatment interventions.

I. Fatourou (✉) • A. Rombotis
Hellenic American University Alumna, Athens, Greece
e-mail: ifatourou@hauniv.edu; arombotis@hauniv.edu

A. Sax (ed.), *Understanding Child Psychopathology Through Fairytales*, https://doi.org/10.1007/978-3-032-14097-5_8

Keywords Adolescence • Social equality • Law • Group membership • Risk factors • Protective factors • Attachment style • Conduct disorder

The Story of Robin Hood

The tale of *Robin Hood*, famed for redistributing wealth from the affluent to the impoverished, dates back to the twelfth century and has been retold in numerous forms throughout history. In Howard Pyle's (1967) retelling, Robin is portrayed as a heroic figure and a champion of social equality. The narrative begins with Robin winning an archery contest, later killing a man in self-defense, and subsequently fleeing to escape the harsh justice of the law. Along his journey, he gathers a band of followers—the Merry Men—united by the shared mission of redistributing wealth from the corrupt and greedy elite to the oppressed poor. The story depicts the wealthy as exploitative and uncharitable, compelling Robin and his companions to challenge authority through deception, clever tactics, and defiance of the sheriff who relentlessly pursues them (Fig. 8.1).

Interestingly, Pyle (1967) also describes Robin as living briefly in a palace close to the king before retreating once again to the sanctuary of Sherwood Forest, where his adventures truly unfold. Despite the richness of the plot, little detail is offered about Robin's upbringing, environmental influences, or psychological development. This chapter aims to explore the possible psychopathology and underlying behavioral drives of Robin Hood, speculating on the circumstances that might have shaped him into both an outlaw and a symbol of social reform.

Demographic Background

Traditional accounts of Robin Hood portray him as an English yeoman, most often associated with Nottinghamshire and the surrounding Sherwood Forest during the medieval period (Pyle, 1967). He is depicted as a highly skilled archer and swordsman, admired for his courage, unwavering loyalty, and strong sense of justice. Many tales describe him as a nobleman or a dispossessed aristocrat forced into a life of outlawry due to unjust laws or political persecution.

Robin's band of Merry Men consists of companions from diverse social standings, representing a broad cross-section of medieval society bonded

Fig. 8.1 Robin Hood

by their common goal of challenging oppression and restoring fairness to the disadvantaged. His interactions with the local peasantry reinforce his image as a benevolent and charismatic leader—beloved by the common folk yet feared by corrupt authorities.

While the legend rarely specifies Robin Hood's exact age, his impulsive decision-making, risk-taking behavior, and willingness to defy authority suggest he may have been in mid-adolescence, likely around 15 or 16 years old. These traits will be explored further in the following sections as part of an analysis of his psychological profile and behavioral motivations.

Psychodynamic Analysis

According to Parritz and Troy (2011), understanding Robin Hood's developmental trajectory requires examining four key domains: emotional, social, cognitive, and physical. Analyzing these aspects helps clarify the factors that may have shaped his personality, behaviors, and life choices.

Robin Hood's emotional development, as depicted in traditional ballads and folklore, is complex and strongly influenced by the socio-cultural context of medieval England. His character expresses a wide range of emotions—from anger and indignation at social injustices to empathy and compassion for marginalized groups. These responses reflect heightened sensitivity to inequality and a strong internal drive toward fairness. Despite the constant adversity of life as an outlaw, Robin shows remarkable resilience, maintaining steadfast loyalty to his cause and fostering camaraderie among the Merry Men. His ability to inspire trust and unity suggests well-developed emotional intelligence and interpersonal skills, though the instability of his lifestyle may also have contributed to episodes of emotional dysregulation.

From a social perspective, Robin Hood is most often depicted as a dispossessed nobleman or member of the lower gentry forced into outlawry by political or social injustice (Pyle, 1967). Growing up within a rigidly stratified and unequal society likely sharpened his awareness of oppression and instilled both resilience and adaptability. His interactions with local peasants, combined with his commitment to redistributing wealth, suggest a capacity for empathy and altruism that transcends personal gain, framing his criminal acts as a form of moral rebellion against corrupt authority.

Robin's cognitive development is characterized by strategic thinking, problem-solving, and an advanced understanding of group dynamics. He demonstrates exceptional planning skills, using the terrain of Sherwood Forest to his advantage in ambushes and evasion. His leadership of the Merry Men, each with specialized abilities, further reflects organizational intelligence and sophisticated communication skills. These traits indicate mature cognitive functioning for his presumed age. However, given the unstable and high-risk environment in which he operated, it is plausible that Robin also faced cognitive challenges, such as impulsivity or occasional difficulty in long-term planning—factors that must be considered when evaluating his psychological profile.

Robin Hood's physical development likely played a major role in shaping his behavior. As an adolescent, he would have experienced increased strength, energy, and impulsivity, all of which could heighten risk-taking and defiance of authority figures. His agility and physical prowess, often emphasized in legend, facilitated his success in archery and combat but may also have emboldened his confrontational approach to injustice. Adolescent hormonal fluctuations can further intensify mood variability and impulsive decision-making, providing a biological context for some of his actions.

The historical and cultural context of the twelfth to thirteenth century also significantly influenced Robin Hood's development (Skoda, 2013). Medieval parenting practices and social norms differed greatly from modern standards. At the time, the impoverished majority lived under harsh conditions imposed by a wealthy elite. Robin's actions—though technically criminal, involving theft, deception, and even murder—were perceived as justifiable, even heroic, because they directly alleviated suffering and challenged an oppressive hierarchy. Understanding his behavior thus requires framing it within the moral and societal values of his era.

Finally, based on Erikson's psychosocial theory of development, Robin Hood appears to be in the stage of Identity versus Role Confusion, typical of adolescence (Erikson, 1968). During this period, individuals seek to define their sense of self while navigating social relationships and societal expectations. Robin's defiance of authority and commitment to a noble cause can be interpreted as efforts to construct a personal identity aligned with justice and fairness. Yet, his oscillation between outlaw, leader, and moral crusader also suggests internal conflict and unresolved role confusion—a struggle to reconcile personal values with the constraints of his social reality.

Risk Factors

Several risk factors may have contributed to Robin Hood's psychological development and the emergence of behaviors considered antisocial by the authorities of his time. First, his socioeconomic background as a member of the lower gentry likely fostered feelings of marginalization and acute awareness of systemic inequality. Though specific details about his early childhood are absent from traditional tales, his premature transition into a life of outlawry suggests the possibility of disrupted caregiving, such as parental absence or neglect, depriving him of secure attachment relationships during formative years.

His environment as an outlaw exposed him to chronic violence, high-risk situations, and frequent confrontations with law enforcement, potentially reinforcing aggressive or antisocial tendencies. Association with his band of Merry Men, who themselves may have engaged in morally ambiguous or deviant acts, could have further normalized criminal behavior and risk-taking. Additionally, the lack of a stable and nurturing attachment figure may have contributed to emotional dysregulation, difficulties with impulse control, and challenges in developing conventional empathy, despite his outward acts of kindness toward the poor.

Traumatic experiences stemming from widespread corruption, exploitation, and economic oppression imposed by the ruling elite likely shaped Robin's worldview, fostering distrust of authority and validating retaliatory actions against perceived oppressors. Moreover, the prevailing cultural values of the medieval period, which often romanticized rebellion against corrupt power structures, may have blurred his understanding of morality and justice, legitimizing his lawlessness as a form of righteousness. Finally, his outlaw status and resulting stigmatization could have amplified feelings of rejection, alienation, and hostility toward mainstream society, further perpetuating defiance and antisocial patterns of behavior.

Protective Factors

Despite these risks, Robin Hood's life and behavior also reflect several protective factors that may have mitigated potential negative developmental outcomes and fostered resilience. Central among these is his strong moral compass, rooted in a personal sense of justice that guided his decisions and distinguished his actions from purely self-serving criminality. His altruistic motives—stealing from the rich to aid the poor—demonstrate enduring empathy, compassion, and prosocial values that counterbalance the harshness of his environment.

Robin's charisma and leadership skills provided him with a supportive social network in the form of the Merry Men, fostering bonds of loyalty, trust, and mutual protection. This sense of belonging likely alleviated feelings of isolation, providing emotional stability and validation of his purpose. His popularity among the common people offered additional social reinforcement, giving him a meaningful identity as a protector of the oppressed.

Psychologically, Robin displayed remarkable resilience and adaptive coping mechanisms, relying on wit, humor, and advanced strategic planning to navigate danger and uncertainty. These skills not only ensured his survival but also bolstered his confidence and ability to lead effectively under pressure. His unwavering commitment to social justice, even at personal risk, reflects strong ethical values and inner fortitude that acted as a buffer against the potentially corrosive effects of trauma, marginalization, and exposure to violence.

Together, these protective factors highlight Robin Hood's capacity for altruism, leadership, and resilience, illustrating how positive traits and social supports can counterbalance adverse circumstances and help shape a figure celebrated as both an outlaw and a folk hero.

Attachment Style

Robin Hood's attachment style can be theorized through an analysis of his interpersonal behaviors, emotional regulation, and relationships, drawing on attachment theory as a framework for understanding adult psychopathology (Shi et al., 2012). Although the traditional tales provide little explicit detail regarding his early caregiving experiences, certain inferences can be made based on his early entrance into a life of outlawry, potential parental absence, and exposure to traumatic social conditions.

The lack of consistent nurturing figures during formative years may have contributed to characteristics of an anxious-avoidant attachment style, marked by ambivalence toward intimacy, fear of rejection, and emotional distancing as a protective mechanism. Prolonged exposure to violence, unpredictability, and betrayal in his environment may also have fostered traits associated with disorganized attachment, including emotional dysregulation, inconsistent relational patterns, and difficulty establishing stable, trusting bonds due to unresolved trauma and internal conflict (Boyd & Bee, 2019).

Despite these potential disruptions, Robin demonstrates the ability to form deep, supportive connections with his band of Merry Men and the local peasantry. His capacity to inspire loyalty and maintain enduring alliances suggests an underlying foundation of secure attachment, characterized by comfort with both closeness and autonomy in relationships. This coexistence of secure, anxious-avoidant, and disorganized tendencies highlights the complex, multifaceted nature of Robin Hood's attachment style, likely shaped by early adversity yet partially mitigated by later experiences of camaraderie and belonging. These mixed patterns may have influenced both his resilience and the emotional challenges evident in his adult behaviors.

Diagnosis and Assessment

Robin Hood's behavioral history, as portrayed in traditional narratives, reflects a persistent pattern of law-breaking, deceit, and aggression that may align with diagnostic criteria for conduct disorder (CD) during adolescence, with potential progression to antisocial personality disorder (ASPD) in adulthood (Nathan & Gorman, 2002).

The accounts begin with Robin being pursued for deer poaching—a violation of contemporary law—followed by acts of homicide in a confrontation, recurrent theft, deception, manipulation of others, and repeated defiance of legal authority (Pyle, 1967). Although these behaviors are often rationalized under the guise of aiding the poor, they remain unlawful and repetitive, fostering a cycle of risk-taking and a perceived immunity to consequences.

According to the DSM-5 (APA, 2013), CD is characterized by a persistent violation of societal norms and the rights of others, manifesting through behaviors such as aggression, destruction of property, deceitfulness, theft, and serious rule violations. Severity is determined by the number of symptoms present: mild (fewer than four), moderate (four to five), or severe (six or more). These patterns typically begin before age 15 and, without intervention, may lead to ASPD in adulthood.

ASPD itself is defined by pervasive disregard for the rights of others, evident through behaviors such as repeated unlawful acts, deceit for personal gain, impulsivity, irritability, aggression, reckless disregard for safety, irresponsibility, and lack of remorse. The individual must be at least 18 years old, with evidence of CD onset before age 15, and the behaviors cannot occur exclusively during schizophrenia or bipolar disorder (APA, 2013).

Robin Hood's actions—frequent aggression toward perceived enemies, chronic defiance of legal authority, manipulative strategies against adversaries, and rationalization of theft and violence—closely align with CD diagnostic features. While his exact age in folklore is ambiguous, these behaviors plausibly originated in adolescence, evolving into a broader antisocial pattern consistent with ASPD traits.

For accurate diagnosis, it is essential to distinguish between developmentally normative adolescent rebellion and clinically significant conduct problems (Parritz & Troy, 2011). A comprehensive, multi-method assessment is recommended, incorporating behavioral observations, self-reports, collateral information from peers or parental figures, and standardized tools such as the Conduct Disorder Questionnaire (Milam, 1998), the Delinquent Activities Scale (Reavy et al., 2014), and the Child Behavior Checklist (Lowe, 1998). Such an approach would allow for nuanced evaluation of the persistence, severity, and functional impairment of Robin Hood's behaviors, aiding in differential diagnosis and consideration of contextual factors influencing his actions.

Etiology

Understanding the etiology of a psychological disorder is essential for accurate diagnosis and effective treatment, as it provides insight into the underlying causes, contributing factors, and developmental pathways influencing the disorder's progression. In Robin Hood's case, multiple biological, cognitive, emotional, and social factors may have contributed to behaviors consistent with CD and potential ASPD in adulthood.

Children raised in environments characterized by neglect, parental rejection, abuse, or exposure to depression and anxiety are at heightened risk of developing CD (Parritz & Troy, 2011). Such early adversities can manifest as irritability, aggression, diminished self-esteem, and heightened anxiety, often serving as precursors to antisocial tendencies later in life (Barry et al., 2013). Robin Hood's early displacement from mainstream society and possible lack of stable parental figures suggest that emotional neglect or rejection may have played a formative role in shaping his behavioral patterns and coping mechanisms.

Individuals with CD or ASPD frequently exhibit emotional dysregulation, attentional difficulties, impulsivity, and, in some cases, delays in cognitive or speech development (Nathan & Gorman, 2002). While there is no explicit evidence of such delays in Robin Hood's folklore narrative, his impulsive decision-making, disregard for authority, and repeated engagement in high-risk behaviors could reflect underlying cognitive processing and regulatory difficulties common in this diagnostic profile. A hereditary predisposition must also be considered, as studies suggest a genetic component to CD and ASPD, with affected parents being more likely to transmit these tendencies to their offspring (Barry et al., 2013). Without early therapeutic intervention, these patterns often escalate in severity over time (Parritz & Troy, 2011).

Socioeconomic disadvantage is strongly correlated with the development of conduct-related disorders. Factors such as poverty, residence in high-crime areas, exposure to deviant peers, and lack of positive role models increase the likelihood of antisocial behaviors (Barry et al., 2013). Robin Hood's status as a marginalized member of the lower gentry and his early immersion in an outlaw lifestyle suggest prolonged exposure to environments where deviant behaviors were normalized, reinforcing maladaptive coping strategies. Furthermore, children frequently internalize behavioral models from their surroundings; repeated exposure to violence or criminal activity during formative years often leads to imitation of these behaviors later in life (Nathan & Gorman, 2002).

Notably, Robin Hood demonstrates an enduring sense of empathy and moral reasoning, particularly in his consistent efforts to aid the oppressed. While this does not negate the presence of antisocial behaviors, it introduces a significant protective factor, suggesting a partially intact moral framework that differentiates him from individuals with more severe, empathy-deficient presentations of CD or ASPD. This capacity for altruism may be crucial in designing a potential treatment or rehabilitative plan, as it provides a foundation upon which prosocial behaviors could be strengthened.

In summary, the likely etiology of Robin Hood's conduct-related psychopathology is multifactorial, encompassing adverse emotional experiences, potential cognitive vulnerabilities, genetic predisposition, and detrimental social environments, partially offset by protective moral and empathetic tendencies. This complex interplay highlights the importance of considering both risk and resilience factors when conceptualizing his psychological profile.

Treatment/Interventions

Prevention is widely regarded as the most effective approach to reducing the onset and severity of CD and its potential progression into ASPD (Offord & Bennett, 1994). Research highlights the importance of early interventions that enhance competency, emotional regulation, and problem-solving skills in children and adolescents (Parritz & Troy, 2011). Many youths with CD experience significant deficits in empathy, often struggling to understand or consider the perspectives of their victims. To address this, prevention programs frequently focus on improving social cognition, moral reasoning, and emotional awareness, with some demonstrating positive outcomes in reducing antisocial tendencies (Nathan & Gorman, 2002). If Robin Hood had been identified as at risk during early childhood and placed in such programs, interventions aimed at fostering self-control, perspective-taking, and non-violent conflict resolution could have altered his developmental trajectory, potentially preventing the escalation of delinquent behaviors in adolescence.

During adolescence, there remains considerable opportunity for behavioral reorganization, though many individuals with CD are resistant to treatment due to mistrust of authority or poor motivation for change. While pharmacological interventions such as mood stabilizers may help manage impulsivity or aggression in some cases, research on medication effectiveness for CD remains limited (Parritz & Troy, 2011). Evidence strongly supports parental involvement in intervention programs, as effective parenting practices are associated with significant reductions in problematic behaviors (Woolfenden et al., 2001). However, even with improvements, many adolescents do not fully achieve normative functioning, highlighting the need for comprehensive, multi-level approaches that address individual, familial, and environmental factors (Bakker et al., 2016).

Community-based strategies are particularly beneficial in addressing conduct-related psychopathology, especially in cases resembling Robin Hood's behaviors. Approaches that integrate adolescents into supportive, structured environments provide alternatives to punitive responses, focusing instead on addressing underlying causes of delinquency. Programs led by community mentors, counselors, or educators can help redirect antisocial tendencies by promoting prosocial activities, developing emotional resilience, and building positive peer networks (Woolfenden et al., 2001). While residential programs or "boot camps" may be effective for some youths, they often depend heavily on individual willingness to engage and may be less appropriate for those with histories of maltreatment or co-occurring internalizing disorders (Parritz & Troy, 2011). In Robin Hood's case, non-punitive, community-oriented interventions emphasizing empathy development, moral reasoning, and restorative justice could have provided a more sustainable pathway to behavioral change.

A systemic approach involving parents, teachers, community leaders, and non-deviant peers is crucial for long-term success. Prevention and treatment programs embedded within mental health services, schools, juvenile justice systems, and community organizations offer the best chance of reshaping developmental pathways away from antisocial conduct. Early identification of risk factors, combined with supportive guidance from trusted adults and access to structured, prosocial opportunities, can significantly reduce the persistence of conduct-disordered behaviors into adulthood.

Conclusion

Robin Hood's actions, including theft, defiance of authority, manipulation, and aggression, closely align with the diagnostic features of CD and suggest the potential for progression to ASPD if left untreated. His behaviors likely emerged from a complex interplay of adverse emotional experiences, environmental risk factors, and possible genetic predisposition, compounded by prolonged exposure to violence, deviance, and social marginalization. While his enduring sense of empathy toward the oppressed provides an important protective factor, it is insufficient on its own to counteract entrenched patterns of delinquency.

A community-based intervention model, focusing on empathy development, emotional regulation, and positive social integration, would be the most appropriate treatment pathway for individuals displaying similar behavioral profiles. This approach emphasizes prevention over punishment and leverages the influence of supportive adults, mentors, and non-deviant peers to foster long-term behavioral change. Implemented across mental health, educational, and community settings, such interventions hold the potential to redirect maladaptive conduct, reduce future antisocial tendencies, and ultimately facilitate reintegration into a constructive, prosocial role within society.

References

American Psychiatric Association. (2013). *Diagnostic and statistical manual of mental disorders* (5th ed.). American Psychiatric Association.

Bakker, M. J., Greven, C. U., Buitelaar, J. K., & Glennon, J. C. (2016). Practitioner review: Psychological treatments for children and adolescents with conduct disorder problems-a systematic review and meta-analysis. *Journal of Child Psychology and Psychiatry, 58*(1), 4–18. https://doi.org/10.1111/jcpp.12590

Barry, C. T., Golmaryami, F. N., Rivera-Hudson, N., & Frick, P. J. (2013). Evidence-based assessment of conduct disorder: Current considerations and

preparation for DSM-5. *Professional Psychology: Research and Practice, 44*(1), 56–63. https://doi.org/10.1037/a0029202
Boyd, D. R., & Bee, H. L. (2019). *Lifespan development.* Pearson.
Erikson, E. H. (1968). *Identity: Youth and crisis.* Norton & Co..
Lowe, L. A. (1998). Using the child behavior checklist in assessing conduct disorder: Issues of reliability and validity. *Research on Social Work Practice, 8*(3), 286–301. https://doi.org/10.1177/104973159800800303
Milam, D. L. (1998). *Conduct disorder questionnaire (Publication No. 1737)* [master's thesis, Marshall University]. Marshall Digital Scholar. https://mds.marshall.edu/etd/1737
Nathan, P., & Gorman, J. M. (2002). *A guide to treatments that work* (1st ed.). Oxford University Press.
Offord, D. R., & Bennett, K. J. (1994). Conduct disorder: Long-term outcomes and intervention effectiveness. *Journal of the American Academy of Child & Adolescent Psychiatry, 33*(8), 1069–1078. https://doi.org/10.1097/00004583-199410000-00001
Parritz, R. H., & Troy, M. F. (2011). *Disorders of childhood: Development and psychopathology.* Wadsworth Cengage Learning.
Pyle, H. (1967). *Some merry adventures of Robin Hood of great renown in Nottinghamshire.* F. Watts.
Reavy, R., Stein, L. A. R., Quina, K., & Paiva, A. L. (2014). Assessing conduct disorder: A new measurement approach. *Journal of Correctional Health Care, 20*(1), 4–17. https://doi.org/10.1177/1078345813505448
Shi, Z., Bureau, J., Easterbrooks, M. A., Zhao, X., & Lyons, R. K. (2012). Childhood maltreatment and prospectively observed quality of early care as predictors of antisocial personality disorder features. *Infant Mental Health Journal, 33*(1), 55–69. https://doi.org/10.1002/imhj.20295
Skoda, H. (2013). Introduction. In *Medieval violence: Physical brutality in Northern France* (pp. 1270–1330). Oxford Historical Monographs. Oxford Academic. https://doi.org/10.1093/acprof:oso/9780199670833.003.0001
Woolfenden, S., Williams, K. J., & Peat, J. (2001). Family and parenting interventions in children and adolescents with conduct disorder and delinquency aged 10–17. *Cochrane Database of Systematic Reviews, 2001*(2), CD003015. https://doi.org/10.1002/14651858.CD003015

Epilogue

Theodoros Tsirigotis
University of South Wales, United Kingdom
European Institute of Counseling and Psychotherapy, Crete, Greece

To encounter child psychopathology through the lens of fairy tales is to engage with the symbolic logic of suffering—a logic that speaks not in categories but in images, repetition, absence, and transformation. This book reminds us that before a child becomes a "case," they are already a character in a story not entirely of their own making.

Through these chapters, we are invited to listen not only to the fictional voices of Dumbo, Hansel, Ariel, and others but also to the archetypal dramas of abandonment, desire, trauma, and hope. The students, under the direction of Dr. Alessandra Sax, did not simply diagnose—they translated; they did not merely apply knowledge—they engaged with meaning.

There is also something inherently democratic in the structure of this book. By empowering undergraduate students to think symbolically and formulate clinical material through narrative, it models a pedagogy of trust and participation. It suggests that reflective depth is not the privilege of experience alone but a potential ignited by careful guidance, authentic curiosity, and a willingness to sit with complexity.

As a psychologist and clinical educator, I find this model of training deeply significant. It restores the imaginative dimension to a field too often reduced to metrics and symptom lists. It cultivates in emerging

A. Sax (ed.), *Understanding Child Psychopathology Through Fairytales*, https://doi.org/10.1007/978-3-032-14097-5

practitioners the capacity to think symbolically, to feel without being overwhelmed, and to wonder without rushing to explanation. These are not luxuries—they are necessities for anyone working with the emotional lives of children.

The psychoanalytic tradition has long taught us that the child's world is not linear but layered, phantasmatic, and encoded. This book honors that insight by placing clinical formulation in dialog with narrative complexity. It offers a quiet but powerful proposition: that diagnosis can coexist with metaphor, and that healing may begin not with certainty but with the willingness to dwell in story.

Beyond its pedagogical and clinical value, this work stands as a symbolic act of care. It reflects a belief that the inner worlds of children matter, that their voices—even fictional, even ancient—deserve to be heard, held, and made sense of. In this sense, the book is not only useful but also ethical. Not only practical but also poetic.

I leave the reader with this invitation: to carry forward the sensibility cultivated here—not only in how we analyze but also in how we accompany. Let us train ourselves to hear the logic of the child's suffering not only through manuals but also through myth. And let us never forget that the clinician, too, must sometimes read between the lines.

Companion Guide for Educators

Further Analyses

This companion created for educators provides instructional guidance, discussion prompts, and key teaching points based on the glossaries covering child developmental psychopathology, parenting styles, typical and atypical development, mental health challenges in children and adolescents, developmental models, and multicultural models of psychopathology. They are designed to help educators plan lessons, highlight core ideas, and encourage critical thinking. It should be noted that this guide is merely a reference and should not be considered as absolute in its entirety.

The following models are additional concepts of child and adolescent development for students to consider for the development of each character from Chaps. 2, 3, 4, 5, 6, 7, 8: Dumbo, Little Red Riding Hood, Pinocchio, Hansel and Gretel, Peter Pan, Ariel, and Robin Hood, as well as other fictional characters for creative clinical practice. Consider the following questions and then utilize the detailed companion guide when teaching your students.

Models of developmental psychopathology: What models of developmental psychopathology would your assessment be based on for your character and/or client?

A. Sax (ed.), *Understanding Child Psychopathology Through Fairytales*, https://doi.org/10.1007/978-3-032-14097-5

Bowlby and Ainsworth's models of attachment: What attachment style do you speculate your character or client has experienced in childhood and adolescence?

Baumrind's parenting styles: According to your character's or client's development and current positive or negative outcomes in his/her life; what type of parenting style could have been implemented in childhood and adolescence?

Typical childhood and adolescent milestones of development: Where is your character and/or client developmentally for his or her age, and what milestones of development have been accomplished?

Atypical childhood and adolescent milestones of development: What are some signs of atypical development in your character's or client's history, and what milestones have not been met thus far in his or her lifespan?

Developmental models: What are the developmental models that you would utilize in assessing and evaluating your character's overall functioning; emotionally, socially, cognitively, and physically?

Models of multicultural psychopathology: Speculate on the important factors of cultural diversity that are applicable to your character's history and presenting problem; what model of multicultural counseling is applicable?

Ego functions and defense mechanisms: Reflect on your character's or client's current behavior and functioning. Which ego functions and defense mechanisms would you assess that your character or client displays?

Developmental Psychopathology

Key Teaching Points

- Differentiate between the variations of clinically significant disorders that children and adolescents manifest.
- Explain the risk and protective factors that affect children's mental health.
- Discuss the concept of resilience and its implications for children and adolescents.

Discussion Prompts

- What are examples of protective factors in school settings?
- How can comorbidity of diagnoses impact treatment?

Suggested Activities

- Case vignette analysis of a child with multiple risk factors.
- Role-play of an interdisciplinary team meeting discussing a child's case (i.e., principal, teacher, school counselor, special educator).

A. Sax (ed.), *Understanding Child Psychopathology Through Fairytales*, https://doi.org/10.1007/978-3-032-14097-5

Typical Versus Atypical Development

Key Teaching Points

- Define typical and atypical development in children and adolescents.
- Identify developmental milestones and possible delays in children and adolescents.
- Recognize the differences between well-adjusted and maladjusted children and adolescents.

Discussion Prompts

- Why is early identification of atypical development critical?
- What are the contributing factors that affect maladjustment in children and adolescents?

Suggested Activities

- Create a timeline from birth to adolescents (0 months to 19 years of age) of all developmental milestones.
- Observation assignment on a preschool-aged child in an early childhood setting.

A. Sax (ed.), *Understanding Child Psychopathology Through Fairytales*, https://doi.org/10.1007/978-3-032-14097-5

Developmental Models

Key Teaching Points

- Compare and contrast the major developmental theories of Piaget, Vygotsky, Freud, Erikson, and Bronfenbrenner.
- Explain continuous versus discontinuous development in children.
- Apply theoretical models of child and adolescent development to classroom and clinical scenarios.

Discussion Prompts

- Which developmental theory best explains learning in early childhood classrooms?
- How does Bronfenbrenner's Ecological Model help explain differences in development among children in the same school?

Suggested Activities

- Group presentations on assigned developmental theories.
- Draw a diagram or concept map to compare two developmental models.

A. Sax (ed.), *Understanding Child Psychopathology Through Fairytales*, https://doi.org/10.1007/978-3-032-14097-5

Mental Health Challenges in Children and Adolescents

Key Teaching Points

- Differentiate between common childhood and adolescent disorders.
- Discuss age-related symptomatology in children and adolescents.
- Understand the importance of early intervention and the steps in this process.

Discussion Prompts

- How might depression appear in a 7-year-old child and a 16-year-old adolescent? Compare and contrast the significant factors affecting both and create flash cards for a group activity.
- What factors contribute to the rise of anxiety disorders in children and adolescents?

A. Sax (ed.), *Understanding Child Psychopathology Through Fairytales*, https://doi.org/10.1007/978-3-032-14097-5

Suggested Activities

- Design five to ten creative, informative brochures for a school about being healthy and well and the specific mental health conditions seen in children and adolescents.
- Analyze a film and/or TV episode that portrays challenges related to child and adolescent mental health.

Companion Guide for Students and Trainees: Child and Adolescent Development, Psychopathology, and Related Models

Note: The following course objectives and learning outcomes are applicable to a child and adolescent psychopathology course on an undergraduate level and can be adapted by educators for graduate and doctoral levels, as well as the provided companion guide.

Course Objectives:

- Provide the opportunity for students to learn about the basic concepts of developmental psychopathology through class discussions, assignments, and role-plays,
- Provide the opportunity for students to understand typical versus atypical patterns of development from early childhood through adolescence, through class discussions, assignments, and role-plays,
- Provide students with knowledge and skills applicable to understanding case conceptualizations, demonstrated through class discussions, role-plays, and assessments.

Learning Outcomes:

- Describe and identify typical developments and features of childhood and adolescent psychiatric disorders through class assignments and activities,
- Understand the personal, situational, environmental, cultural, and interactional factors that contribute to atypical development and

A. Sax (ed.), *Understanding Child Psychopathology Through Fairytales*, https://doi.org/10.1007/978-3-032-14097-5

psychological disorders in children and adolescents through class discussions and role-plays,
- Examine some of the methods that are used to treat and prevent psychological disturbances and enhance the positive development of children and adolescents through participation in class discussion, class assignments, and class role-plays.

This companion guide consolidates key terms on child developmental psychopathology, parenting styles, typical and atypical development, mental health challenges in children and adolescents, developmental models, and multicultural models of psychopathology. It is designed to assist students and developing trainees to better understand, review, and apply core concepts in developmental psychopathology.

Child Developmental Psychopathology

Child Developmental Psychopathology—The study of the origins, development, and progression of mental disorders in children and adolescents.

Comorbidity—The co-occurrence of two or more disorders in the same individual.

Protective Factor—A condition in an individual's environment that reduces the likelihood or impact of a disorder during childhood and adolescence.

Resilience—The ability to adapt positively despite adversity in life.

Risk Factor—A condition in an individual's environment that increases the likelihood of developing a disorder during childhood and adolescence.

References

Parritz, R. H., & Troy, M. F. (2011). *Disorders of childhood: Development and psychopathology*. Wadsworth Cengage Learning.

Parenting Styles

Authoritarian—Low in warmth and high in control; linked to negative outcomes in children and adolescents.

Authoritative—High in warmth and control; linked to positive outcomes in children and adolescents.

Neglectful—Low in warmth and control; linked to severe negative outcomes in childhood and adolescence.

Permissive—High in warmth and low in control; linked to less positive outcomes in children and adolescents.

References

Baumrind D. (1978). Parental disciplinary patterns and social competence in children. *Youth & Society*, *9*, 239–267. https://doi.org/10.1177/0044118X7800900302

Typical Versus Atypical Development

Atypical Development—Development that occurs outside the expected norms and can possibly be indicative of a disorder.

Delay—Slower than expected attainment of developmental milestones.

Developmental Milestone—A skill or ability that most children achieve by a specific age.

Regression—The loss of a previously acquired skill.

Typical Development—The progression of skills and abilities within expected age ranges of lifespan development.

References

Boyd, D. R., & Bee, H. L. (2019). *Lifespan development*. Pearson.
Parritz, R. H., & Troy, M. F. (2011). *Disorders of childhood: Development and psychopathology*. Wadsworth Cengage Learning.

Mental Health Challenges in Children

Anxiety Disorders—Excessive fear or worry affecting overall functioning.

Attention-Deficit Hyperactivity Disorder—Patterns of inattention, hyperactivity, or impulsivity causing impairment in personal and occupational functioning.

Autism Spectrum Disorder—Difficulties in social communication and interpersonal relationships, along with restricted/repetitive behaviors that affect personal and occupational functioning.

Conduct Disorder—Purposeful malintent toward people and animals, often breaking rules and laws in home, school, or society.

Depression—Persistent sadness and loss of interest in activities.

Oppositional Defiant Disorder—Defiant and hostile behavior toward authority figures.

References

American Psychiatric Association (APA). (2013). *Diagnostic and statistical manual of mental disorders* (5th ed.). American Psychiatric Association.

Models

Bandura's Social Learning Theory—Learning through observing and imitating others (children with parents, caregivers, and teachers).

Bronfenbrenner's Ecological Systems Theory—Multiple environmental systems that shape child development within five systems: microsystem, mesosystem, exosystem, macrosystem, and chronosystem.

Erikson's Psychosocial Theory—Eight life stages with key conflicts to resolve: trust versus mistrust (0–18 months), autonomy versus shame and doubt (18 months to 3 years), initiative versus guilt (3–5 years), industry versus inferiority (6–11 years), identity versus role confusion (12–18 years), intimacy versus isolation (18–40 years), generativity versus stagnation (40–65 years), and integrity versus despair (65 years and older).

Piaget's Cognitive Development Theory—Four stages of cognitive processes from infancy to adulthood: sensorimotor stage (birth to 2 years), preoperational (2–7 years), concrete (7–11 years), and formal (11 years and older) operation stages.

Vygotsky's Sociocultural Theory—Learning through social interaction and cultural contexts.

References

Boyd, D. R., & Bee, H. L. (2019). *Lifespan development*. Pearson.

Parritz, R. H., & Troy, M. F. (2011). *Disorders of childhood: Development and psychopathology*. Wadsworth Cengage Learning.

Multicultural Models of Psychopathology

Acculturation—Adaptation to a new culture with positive adjustment.

Culture-Bound Syndromes—Mental disorders unique to specific cultures.

Cultural Competence—Ability to work effectively with clients from diverse cultures and backgrounds.

Cultural Relativism—Understanding behavior in the context of the person's culture.

Minority Identity Model—Impact of discrimination and mental health of marginalized groups of people.

Racial, Cultural, and Identity Development Model—A racial/cultural development model that attempts to integrate the racial/cultural development of groups of color.

White Racial Identity Development—The process with accompanying stages or phases by which White individuals achieve their racial identity.

Worldview—People's attitudes, beliefs, and values that affect cognitions, decisions, and behaviors in how they understand the world they live in.

References

Sue, D. W., Sue, D., Neville, H., & Smith, L. (2019). *Counseling the culturally diverse: Theory and practice* (8th ed.). Wiley.

Practice Guide of Ego Functions and Defense Mechanisms

This guide explains some of the common key ego functions and defense mechanisms in psychoanalytic theory. It is designed for students and practitioners to recognize how the ego mediates between internal drives, external reality, and moral constraints.

Ego Functions

Defensive Functioning—Use of defense mechanisms to manage anxiety and conflict.

Judgment—Ability to assess situations and anticipate consequences.

Impulse Control—Ability to manage and delay urges and impulses.

Object Relations—Ability to form and maintain healthy relationships with others.

Reality Testing—The capacity to distinguish between internal thoughts and external reality.

Regulation of Affect, Drives, and Impulses—Capacity to modulate emotional responses and impulses appropriately.

Synthetic Integrative Functioning—Integrating conflicting thoughts, emotions, or experiences into a coherent whole.

Thought Processes—Logical and coherent thinking.

A. Sax (ed.), *Understanding Child Psychopathology Through Fairytales*, https://doi.org/10.1007/978-3-032-14097-5

Defense Mechanisms

Compensation—Overachieving in one area to make up for shortcomings in another.

Denial—Refusing to accept reality or facts.

Displacement—Redirecting emotions from a threatening target to a safer one.

Identification—Adopting the characteristics of another person or group.

Intellectualization—Focusing on abstract or factual details to avoid emotional distress.

Projection—Attributing one's own unacceptable thoughts or feelings to another.

Rationalization—Offering logical explanations for behaviors driven by unconscious impulses.

Reaction Formation—Behaving in a way opposite to one's unacceptable thoughts or feelings.

Regression—Reverting to behaviors characteristic of an earlier developmental stage.

Repression—Keeping distressing thoughts unconscious.

Splitting—Viewing people or situations as all good or all bad.

Sublimation—Channeling unacceptable impulses into socially acceptable activities.

Suppression—Consciously choosing to delay paying attention to a thought or emotion.

Undoing—Trying to reverse or undo feelings by engaging in contrary behavior.

References

Goldstein, E. (1984). *Ego psychology and social work practice*. The Free Press.

Glossary

Academic Achievement—School performance influenced by home environment and parental involvement.

Adolescent Mental Health—The emotional, psychological, and social well-being of individuals aged approximately 12–19 years.

Anxiety Disorders—Excessive fear or worry interfering with daily life (e.g., generalized anxiety disorder, social anxiety disorder).

Attachment Theory—Focuses on the bonds between children and caregivers and their impact on development.

Attention-Deficit/Hyperactivity Disorder—Ongoing pattern of inattention, hyperactivity, and/or impulsivity.

Authoritarian Parenting—Low responsiveness + high demandingness. Characterized by strict rules, high expectations, and limited warmth. Outcome: Associated with obedience but lower happiness and self-esteem.

Authoritative Parenting—High responsiveness + high demandingness. Characterized by warmth, clear rules, and supportive discipline. Outcome: Often linked to high self-esteem, academic success, and social competence.

Baumrind's Parenting Typology—Diana Baumrind's influential classification of parenting styles: authoritative, authoritarian, and permissive.

Behavioral Problems—Disruptive or maladaptive behaviors possibly linked to certain parenting styles.

A. Sax (ed.), *Understanding Child Psychopathology Through Fairytales*, https://doi.org/10.1007/978-3-032-14097-5

Bipolar Disorder—Episodes of depression alternating with mania/hypomania.

Bronfenbrenner's Ecological Systems Theory—Explains development through multiple environmental systems, from immediate surroundings to broader cultural influences.

Child Development—Changes in physical, cognitive, social, and emotional functioning that occur from conception through adolescence and result from the interaction of biological and environmental influences.

Child Mental Health—The emotional, psychological, and social well-being of children, affecting how they think, feel, and behave.

Collectivism—A social pattern consisting of closely linked individuals who see themselves as part of one or more collectives.

Community-Based Approaches—Programs delivered within specific cultural communities to improve accessibility and trust.

Continuous Development—Gradual and cumulative developmental changes without distinct stages.

Coping Skills—Strategies children use to manage stress, emotions, and challenges.

Crisis Intervention—Immediate support during acute mental health emergencies.

Critical Period—A specific time during which development must occur for certain abilities to emerge.

Cultural Competence—The ability of mental health professionals to effectively work within the cultural context of the client.

Cultural Norms—Shared values and expectations that shape parenting practices.

Cultural Sensitivity—Awareness and respect for cultural differences in beliefs, practices, and communication styles.

Culturally Adapted Interventions—Mental health treatments modified to align with the client's cultural context.

Depression—Persistent sadness, irritability, or loss of interest in activities.

Developmental Milestones—Observable skills or abilities that most individuals achieve by a certain age.

Developmental Model—A theoretical framework explaining how and why individuals change over time.

Developmental Psychopathology—An approach to understanding the origins and course of individual patterns of behavioral maladaptation by integrating knowledge from developmental psychology, clinical psychology, and psychiatry.

Dismissive-Avoidant Attachment—Involves emotional distance, self-reliance, and discomfort with closeness, often linked to rejecting or neglectful caregivers.

Discontinuous Development—Development occurring in distinct stages or steps.

Disruptive Mood Dysregulation Disorder—Chronic irritability and frequent temper outbursts.

DSM-5—Diagnostic and Statistical Manual used to classify and diagnose mental disorders and patterns of behaviors.

Early Intervention—Support provided to children at the first signs of a problem.

Emotional Regulation—The ability to monitor, evaluate, and adjust emotional responses to situations.

Erikson's Psychosocial Theory—Outlines eight stages of psychosocial development, each with a central conflict to resolve.

Family History—Mental health issues in parents or relatives increasing risk.

Family Therapy—Therapy involving parents and siblings to improve relationships.

Fearful-Avoidant (Disorganized) Attachment—Combines desire for closeness with fear of intimacy, often linked to trauma, abuse, or loss in early relationships.

Freud's Psychosexual Theory—Suggests development occurs through five stages focused on different erogenous zones.

Generalized Anxiety Disorder—Chronic, excessive worry across multiple situations.

Help-Seeking Behavior—How and when individuals seek mental health support, shaped by cultural norms.

Individualism—A social pattern consisting of loosely linked individuals who view themselves as independent of collectives.

Maccoby and Martin's Model—An expanded model adding the neglectful style to Baumrind's original three.

Major Depressive Disorder—Severe form of depression with symptoms lasting at least two weeks.

Mental Disorder—A clinically significant disturbance in a child's cognition, emotion regulation, or behavior.

Mental Health Challenge—A difficulty or condition affecting a child's emotional, behavioral, or cognitive functioning.

Multicultural Psychopathology—The study and understanding of mental disorders through the lens of diverse cultural contexts.

Nature Versus Nurture—The debate over the influence of genetics (nature) and environment (nurture) on development.

Neglectful (Uninvolved) Parenting—Low responsiveness + low demandingness. Characterized by minimal interaction and guidance. Outcome: Often associated with poor academic and social outcomes.

Parental Demandingness (Control)—The extent to which parents set expectations, monitor behavior, and enforce rules.

Parental Responsiveness (Warmth)—The degree of support, affection, and acceptance a parent shows toward their child.

Parenting Style—A consistent pattern of attitudes, behaviors, and emotional climate in which parents raise their children.

Permissive Parenting—High responsiveness + low demandingness. Characterized by indulgence, few rules, and avoidance of confrontation. Outcome: Linked to impulsivity and poor self-regulation.

Play Therapy—Using play to help children express feelings and resolve problems.

Positive Parenting—An approach emphasizing warmth, encouragement, and skill-building over punishment.

Protective Factors—Conditions such as supportive relationships and stable environments that reduce risk.

Psychoeducation—Teaching children and families about the condition and coping strategies.

Reactive Attachment Disorder—A condition in which a child fails to form healthy emotional bonds with caregivers, often due to severe neglect or abuse, characterized by withdrawal and lack of responsiveness.

Resilience—The process of adapting well in the face of adversity, trauma, tragedy, threats, or significant sources of stress.

Risk Factors—Characteristics, conditions, or behaviors that increase the likelihood of the occurrence of a disease or injury.

School-Based Supports—Interventions provided in educational settings to assist students in their learning.

Secure Attachment—A form of attachment in which infants use the caregiver as a secure base from which to explore and show pleasure upon reunion.

Self-Harm—Deliberate injury to oneself as a coping mechanism.

Self-Regulation—The ability to manage emotions, thoughts, and behaviors.

Sensitive Period—A time when development is most responsive to environmental influences.

Social Competence—The ability to interact effectively and harmoniously with others.

Socialization—The process of learning norms, values, and behaviors of a society.

Socioeconomic Status (SES)—Economic and social conditions influencing parenting resources and stress levels.

Stages of Development—Distinct phases of growth and change in physical, cognitive, social, and emotional domains.

Stigma—Negative attitudes or discrimination toward individuals with mental illness, influenced by society and cultural beliefs.

Suicidal Ideation—Thoughts or plans of taking one's own life.

Recommended Reading

Beauchaine, T. P., & Hinshaw, S. P. (Eds.). (2017). *Child and adolescent psychopathology*. John Wiley & Sons.

Bornstein, M. H. (2012). Cultural approaches to parenting, *Parenting: Science and Practice*, *12*(2–3), 212–221. https://doi.org/10.1080/15295192.2012.683359

Cassidy, J., & Shaver, S. (Eds.) (2018). *Handbook of attachment: Theory, research and clinical applications*. Guilford Press.

Cicchetti, D. (Ed.) (2016). *Developmental psychopathology, theory and method* (Vol. 1). John Wiley & Sons.

Cicchetti, D. (Ed.). (2016). *Developmental psychopathology, developmental neuroscience* (Vol. 2). John Wiley & Sons.

Israel, A. C., Malatras, J., W., & Wicks-Nelson, R. (2020). *Abnormal child and adolescent psychology* (9th ed.). Routledge.

Johnson, L. V. K. (2016). The positive impacts of fairy tales for children. *English 345*, *14*, 77-81.

Harris, P. L., de Rosnay, M., & Ronfard, S. (2013). The mysterious emotional life of little red riding hood. *Contributions to Human Development*, *26*, 106–118. https://doi.org/10.1159/000354364

Kordi, A., & Baharudin, R. (2010). Parenting attitude and style and its effect on children's school achievements. *International Journal of Psychological Studies*, *2*(2). https://doi.org/10.5539/ijps.v2n2p217

A. Sax (ed.), *Understanding Child Psychopathology Through Fairytales*, https://doi.org/10.1007/978-3-032-14097-5

Koutsompou, V. E. (2016). The child and the fairytale: The psychological perspective of children's literature. *International Journal of Languages, Literature and Linguistics, 4*, 213–218.

Lauer, G. (2015). How culture shapes the reading of fairy tales: A cross-cultural approach. *Comparative Literature Studies*. https://doi.org/10.5325/complitstudies.52.4.0663

Lightfoot, C., Cole, M., & Cole, S. (2018). *The development of children* (8th ed.). Worth Publishers.

Phares, V. (2020). *Understanding abnormal child psychology* (4th ed.). Wiley.

Rathus, S. A. (2021). *Childhood voyages in development. International edition* (7th ed.). Cengage.

Williams, J. (2020). *Discover the truly Grim history behind the fairytale of Hansel and Gretel*. https://allthatsinteresting.com

Wilkes, J. (2018). What fairy tales contribute to children's and adolescents mental health. *Televizion*, 48–51.

Wohlfarth, D., & Morgan, R. K. (2017). *Case studies in child and adolescent psychopathology*. Waveland Press.

FSC
www.fsc.org
MIX
Papier | Fördert gute Waldnutzung
FSC® C083411

Kolibri 360 GmbH
Ferdinand-Jühlke-Straße 7
99095 Erfurt, Deutschland
produktsicherheit@kolibri360.de